Also by Helen Humphreys

And
a Dog
Called Fig

Solitude, Connection,
the Writing Life

And
a Dog
Called Fig

Helen Humphreys

Farrar, Straus and Giroux   New York

Farrar, Straus and Giroux
120 Broadway, New York 10271

Excerpt from "Bedfellows" by E.B. White is copyright © by
E.B. White. Reprinted in *E.B. White on Dogs*, edited by
Martha White. Reprinted by permission of ICM Partners. Excerpt
from the story "The Dog That Bit People" by James Thurber is
from *My Life and Hard Times*, copyright © 1933 by Rosemary A.
Thurber. Reprinted by arrangement with Rosemary A. Thurber
and the Barbara Hogenson Agency.

Illustration credits can be found on pages 251–253.

Library of Congress Cataloging-in-Publication Data
Names: Humphreys, Helen, 1961– author.
Title: And a dog called Fig : solitude, connection, the writing life / Helen
  Humphreys.
Description: First American edition. | New York : Farrar, Straus and Giroux,
  2022. | Includes bibliographical references. | Summary: "Poet and novelist Helen
  Humphreys's *And a Dog Called Fig*, a meditation on the benefits of dogs to the
  creative life, including the dogs of well-known writers from history, portraits
  of all the dogs from the author's life, and the arrival and raising of her new
  puppy"— Provided by publisher.
Identifiers: LCCN 2021049038 | ISBN 9780374603885 (hardcover)
Subjects: LCSH: Humphreys, Helen, 1961– | Authors, Canadian—20th century—
  Biography. | Dog owners—Biography. | Dogs. | Human-animal relationships. |
  Authorship—Psychological aspects. | LCGFT: Autobiographies
Classification: LCC PR9199.3.H822 Z46 2022 | DDC 813/.54 [B]—dc23/eng/
  20211102
LC record available at https://lccn.loc.gov/2021049038

Our books may be purchased in bulk for promotional, educational, or business
use. Please contact your local bookseller or the Macmillan Corporate and
Premium Sales Department at 1-800-221-7945, extension 5442, or by
email at MacmillanSpecialMarkets@macmillan.com.

www.fsgbooks.com
www.twitter.com/fsgbooks • www.facebook.com/fsgbooks

1   3   5   7   9   10   8   6   4   2

For my dog pack

I started Early—Took my Dog—

—Emily Dickinson

CONTENTS

BEGINNINGS

Into my writer's isolation will come a dog, to sit beside my chair or to lie on the couch while I work, to force me outside for a walk, and suddenly, although still lonely, this writer will have a companion.

I'm ten years older than when I brought home my last dog, Charlotte, and I hope I have it in me to be there for one more vizsla.

Like my grandmother and my father, I have become attached to one specific breed and cannot imagine living with a different type of dog. I have spent twenty-two consecutive years with vizslas. This will be my third one. I love their joyful, exuberant energy and the close attachment they seek with their humans.

I have forgotten much about living with a puppy, but I do have a dim recollection that it is all-consuming, and that a quiet, contemplative writing life is almost impossible to balance with the chaotic energy of a young dog. So, I am thinking that while my life is upended by the puppy, it might be a good opportunity to write about that experience—to think about my writing life in relation to the dogs I have lived with, and to explore other writers' relationships with their dogs. What does a dog bring to the writing life? My writing life has mostly included dogs, but I have never spent time thinking about what this has meant to my creative journey.

While working on a novel would be difficult with a young dog around, because it requires so much time and attention, surely I should be able to keep a journal with some hastily scratched entries, written in the moments when the puppy is napping or playing?

December 15

When I purchased a puppy before, I usually knew which one I was getting, as the breeder picked the puppy out for me based on my temperament and the temperament of the baby dog—a kind of matchmaking. Each puppy in these previous litters was wearing a little nylon cord collar in a particular colour so they could be easily identified. Hazel was the "yellow" puppy. Charlotte was "green." Violet was "red."

But the new breeder doesn't like the collars, says they just get caught on things, so he hasn't marked the puppies. Also, he maintains that you can't really tell anything about the dogs when they are seven weeks old, and that they will all be fine, decent dogs, no matter which one I am given. I can see his point, and admire his confidence in his breeding program, but it does lend a certain randomness to what seems a significant decision, and I feel unsettled by his attitude. I worry that I might get the wrong dog.

I haven't specified what sex of dog I want, but the litter is mostly female. The puppies were born on October 27, which also happens to be Sylvia Plath's birthday.

Just as picking a title for a book is either easy—in that it occurs right away, sometimes before the book has even been started—or impossible—meaning that no title seems right, ever—so it is for the naming of a dog. "Hazel" was decided before the puppy was brought home. The colour that is hazel is roughly the shade of a vizsla's coat and eyes. Also, at the time it felt unique, not being a popular name for either human or canine. Those were the reasons we picked it for the puppy and it always seemed right, although children had trouble with it and Hazel was sometimes called "Weasel" by anyone under the age of ten.

"Charlotte" was one of dozens of names that I tried out on the new puppy in the weeks after she was living with me. Before she was Charlotte, she was Rosie, Wallis, Harris, and a dozen other names that I can no longer remember. I settled on "Charlotte" because it seemed a vaguely aristocratic name and the puppy had a rather imperious quality to her.

This time, I want a name that isn't a human name at all but is a piece of nature. I have tried and discarded various trees—Ash, Maple, Rowan, Larch. For a while, I was thinking of Cricket, and then Clover, but both names are hard to yell, feel too much of a mouthful for the countless times I will be trying to call the dog away from rolling ecstatically in the guts of a dead fish, or eating fresh, steaming piles of horseshit, or swimming out into the middle of the lake after ducks.

In the end, I'm not the one who thinks of the name. My stepdaughter, in a moment of clairvoyance, texts that she wants the dog to be born on her birthday (which it nearly was) and proclaims that it should be called Fig.

I like the name for its clarity and for how easy it is to say emphatically, and also for the possibility of using it in different ways—Figgy, Figlet. (I amuse myself by making up lots of nicknames for my dogs. In the last year of her life, I hardly ever called Charlotte by her real name, but instead was calling her mostly Joe or Fred. I had tired of her original name, and it didn't really matter what I called her because she and I understood each other without words). So, "Fig" seems good, right. Also, the vizsla, with its dark red fur somewhat resembles the colour of a ripe Calimyrna fig.

Charlotte has been dead for five months and I miss her constantly. The months of being without a dog have been hard. The house has been so empty. Walking has felt pointless. So, I am anxious to fill my life, and my home, with a new dog.

A close friend and I drive north with a blanket and a small crate, in case the puppy is frantic at being separated from her family and needs to be contained for the ride home. Puppy Hazel was desperate to escape from the car when we first picked her up, and I don't want the new puppy to squirm out of my arms. I have memories of a family vacation when I was a child where one of our cats crawled under the accelerator pedal while my father was driving on a busy highway and he almost crashed the car.

I have bought a few new things for the puppy—a soft collar for her little puppy neck, a small coat for winter—but most of what she needs will be provided courtesy of Charlotte. The new dog will eat out of the bowls that my old dog ate from. She will play with the toys that Charlotte left behind. And she will wear Charlotte's old leather collar when she is big enough, because there is still a lot of life left in that collar. Why buy something new when what is already here will work perfectly well? The puppy will be herself, but she will enter into a continuum of dog where much has already been tried and proven.

We left early, but when we arrive at the breeder's, two other families are already here, picking up their puppies. There are six in the litter altogether, four females and two males. One of the females has already been flown out to British Columbia, and the two families that are here with us are taking the males, which leaves three little female puppies writhing in the puppy box on the kitchen floor.

Vizslas are not known for being calm dogs and I fear that Charlotte, in her divine calmness, was an anomaly, but I am ever hopeful. We choose the puppy that seems the quietest and is keen to make eye contact with us. The other two are busy wrestling, and the breeder has already referred to one of them as a "firecracker," which is not appealing. Because the vizsla is a finely tuned hunting dog, they can be neurotic and the line between "high-strung" and flat-out nuts is quite thin. I am confident that I can provide a peaceful environment for a dog, but it helps if the puppy I'm starting out with is not too hyperactive.

On the ride home, it seems that we have chosen well. Mary Louise drives and I sit in the back seat with the puppy, who dozes on my lap or lies in her crate with the door open, snoozing. She seems perfect and I am thankful, but I soon discover she was probably just stunned from the change in environment. Once home, she turns into a clawing, biting machine and draws significant blood from me three times in the first twenty-four hours. Also, the crate—which she didn't mind in the car—she hates in the house. She vocalizes in a high-pitched puppy shriek whenever I put her in there for the briefest of periods to start the crate-training process. (Despite many dog-training books and videos saying otherwise, no dog of mine has ever taken immediately to their crate and thought of it as a "den" or "safe space." Mostly they have objected to being locked in there and separated from the people and action of the household.)

I sleep on the couch with Fig the first night, because I don't want my neighbours to suffer the screams of the puppy captive in her "safe space." Whenever she wakes, I take her outside and we stand in the icy yard—me waiting for Fig to pee or poo, and her shocked by the sudden cold and not knowing why I have brought her outdoors to freeze.

She is unbelievably small—the size of a hiking boot and barely ten pounds—and I almost step on her a dozen times because she is constantly underfoot in her confusion at being separated from her mother and siblings. Seven weeks seems very different from eight weeks, which was the age that Charlotte and Violet and Hazel came home with me. Fig at seven weeks seems more timid and feral than my previous dogs. During the night, she has two modes—biting and sleeping—and she swings between them every couple of hours. When morning comes and I know my neighbours are awake, I throw her in the crate for half an hour while I go to the bathroom and make coffee and tend to my wounds.

I am not feeling confident in my decision to get a puppy. What was I thinking? (I did first look for an adult dog, but because I was stuck on the vizsla, an adult was impossible to find. The dogs are much more in demand now than they were when I had my first vizsla, and there is always a waiting list for puppies, and nary an adult that needs rehoming.) But, in one of the many sleepless moments of the night, I really felt that I had made a terrible mistake and that I wasn't up to the task of having a puppy. I am almost sixty. What if I just don't have the energy to keep up with the physical demands of a young dog? How had I not remembered how incredibly sharp and dangerous those puppy teeth are? Because the puppy brain is a much smaller, simpler one than an adult dog brain, the puppy views biting as play and won't be deterred by the yelps I emit to teach Fig bite inhibition.

I can't tell much about who Fig is in the first twenty-four hours. Her hackles rise at the sound of a crow in the yard. She hides from the postman's knock at the door and is afraid of a visiting dog. She crawls up onto my shoulders to escape what she fears, and her claws rake my face and neck. Blood drips down from three different punctures on my nose, cheek, and neck.

I try not to compare a seven-week-old puppy to my beloved Charlotte, but the puppy just makes me long for my former dog and her calm benevolence. The puppy doesn't seem to be related to anything I know of as "dog," but is instead a wild, unknowable demon.

Fig at seven weeks

With the addition of Fig to my life, I am suddenly trapped and isolated. When the puppy isn't biting, or standing perplexed in the backyard waiting for me to take her back in, she is sleeping on me, making it impossible for me even to get myself a glass of water. That first night, I went eight hours before I could manage to drink anything, and I was light-headed from dehydration.

We have been together for only twenty-four hours and already I feel defeated.

WHEN I WAS STARTING OUT as a writer, I thought that writing would be something that I could learn and then apply, that there would be an end point to the learning, a place at which to arrive. After writing a certain number of novels, say three or four, I would be good at novels and not so much effort would be required to keep writing them. But, of course, that assumption was completely wrong. Writing is not simply about learning skills. Each new novel requires that everything be learned all over again, because no two books are alike, and there are different sets of problems requiring different solutions when creating each one.

But at the beginning, there was no way to know this. And at the beginning of my writing, and my life journey, there was a dog.

My parents acquired a dog before they had a baby. Not because they wanted to use the dog to practise caring for another creature before graduating to having a human child, but because that was the order in which they wanted what they wanted. First a dog, and secondly, a baby.

By the time I was born, Lisa was firmly ensconced in the small house south of London, in Surrey, that my parents had bought upon marrying. A smooth-coated

St. Bernard, she was 150 pounds, weighing more than either my mother or father, and occupying a role, for me, as a third parent. She had puppies while I was learning to walk, each one named after a character in one of the operas that my father loved. I have vague memories of Figaro or Bonzo tugging at my dress, knocking me over, as I manoeuvred unevenly across the rectangle of clipped grass out back of the house. My mother told me later that the puppies would try to steal my toys, sticking their heads through the bars of my playpen, so that I was forced to lie on top of my things instead of playing with them, to protect them from the marauding beasts.

My memories of that house in England are few and foggy. I was very young when we emigrated to Canada, not even three, but while I don't have clear recall of incidents, I do have memories of sensations—the shapes of birds moving in the sky outside my bedroom window, the weight of the cat lying on me in the pram, the spring light on the grass, the softness of English rain.

Lisa walked up the wooden gangway ahead of us onto the steamer ship to Canada. Because she was so large, she didn't fit in the standard pet cages on board. She was allowed to wander freely up on the crew deck, where she was very popular with the shipboard workers, who fed her scraps from their meals. Lisa gained ten pounds during the voyage, one for every day we were at sea.

It had been my father's idea to emigrate. He was between accountancy jobs, and he remembered his own father's dream of moving to Canada. (His father had been killed during World War II, so was never able to actualize his plan.) My mother was in her early twenties and was up for the adventure of the emigration. Lisa and I had no choice in the matter.

In our new suburban house on the edge of Toronto, I would wake in the mornings and go downstairs to the living room, where Lisa slept on a sheepskin rug in front of the fireplace. I would lie up against her belly—I remember that I fit exactly between her two sets of paws. I never went into my parents' room in the morning, but always went to lie with the dog. I think I considered myself to be one of her puppies, but I wonder too if she was a better reminder of England for me than my parents were. A dog's paws will smell of grass, even in winter, so perhaps Lisa simply smelled of home.

The jolt of the immigration, where suddenly all the familiar faces had been replaced by strangers, afflicted me with a shyness so acute that if anyone other than a member of my immediate family talked to me, I would lie on the ground and scream until they went away.

I took refuge in the company of Lisa and in books. My two favourites were dog books. The first was *The Observer's Book of Dogs*, part of the Observer's natural history series published by Frederick Warne & Co., which also released the Beatrix Potter books—both series shared the same tiny format. The first of the Observer's books was *Birds*, published in 1937. *The Observer's Book of Dogs* was published in 1945 and was number eight in the series, after *British Grasses, Sedges and Rushes*, and before *Horses and Ponies*. The dog book was written by Clifford L.B. Hubbard, a Welshman who worked in kennels as a young man while compiling information about the history of dog breeds and writing various books on them. Later, he worked in the book department of Harrods and, later still, ran his own bookshop in Derbyshire. His nickname was "Doggie" and he sometimes wrote articles on dogs for newspapers and magazines using the pseudonym "Canis."

My copy of *The Observer's Book of Dogs* was missing the original dust jacket. It had red boards for a cover and simple black lettering, with the word *DOGS* in large print. The Observer's books, like the Beatrix Potter books, were meant for the small hands of children, and the size of the book was one of the things I liked best about it. I would often look at it under the covers in bed with a flashlight, when I was no longer meant to be reading, and it was small enough to quickly tuck under my pillow, should an adult ascend the stairs towards my room.

Each page of the book contained a photograph or drawing of a particular breed of dog and then a physical description that included historical detail. All the illustrations were in black and white. Years later, I met an ornithologist who had first learned about birds from *The Observer's Book of Birds*, which also had only black and white illustrations. He had gone on to study mostly black and white birds—terns, gulls, kittiwakes—a congruence he had somehow failed to notice until I pointed it out to him.

I liked to look at the photographs of the dogs in the field guide and try to memorize the breeds. The words didn't matter as much to me as the pictures, and perhaps this was because the words, when I read them now, seem designed for adults. I still have the little book with its red cover, and when I look up the breed vizsla there, it is described as "admirably suited to the game and conditions of the puszta. . . ." I would have skated right over that word as a child, but when I look it up now, I find that a *puszta* is a vast Hungarian grassland that was once home to wild horses. While liking to run on woodland trails or go swimming, all of my dogs have loved noodling around a field best of all, which gives me respect for the expertise of Clifford Hubbard.

My second favourite book was much more narrative. Published in 1924, *Dogs You'd Like to Meet* comprised a series of short accounts about heroic dogs that the author, Rowland Johns, had known personally. There was the story of a dog who was caught by his collar in a thicket and couldn't escape, and how a nearby farm dog brought him food every day for two weeks before he was rescued, going hungry himself to help his friend. There was the tale of a dog who had saved his family from a house fire. Other stories presented dogs rescuing humans from drowning, or successfully fighting off bears and wolves. Each short tale was accompanied by a photograph of the heroic dog, lending credibility to the whole enterprise. It was hard to disbelieve an account of canine bravery when there was a photograph of the actual dog in question.

These dogs were, indeed, dogs I would have liked to meet. They were presented as having personalities, likes and dislikes, fears and joys, in much the same way that the human characters were presented in the other books I was reading. The dogs were people, and I don't think I saw any real difference between dogs and people in terms of their individuality. Certainly, I never thought of dogs as being subordinate to humans, as being lesser.

My mother used to tell us the story of how Lisa's father had been a mountain rescue dog in Switzerland and had saved a handful of people who had been buried in avalanches. My mother had a Christmas card with his portrait painted on it. He had been a famous dog during his lifetime. I always thought he could have been one of the heroic dogs in *Dogs You'd Like to Meet*. We also had the little wooden barrel that he'd worn around his neck when he went out to find the avalanche victims. My mother had been friends with his owners and she had been given the barrel after the dog died. The barrel would have been filled with brandy for the rescues, and my brother and I liked to open it and sniff it, because there was still the faint whiff of alcohol in the tiny wooden cask all those years later.

We also tried to make Lisa wear the barrel, but she wasn't keen on it and successfully resisted our many efforts. She would, however, wear the leather harness that my mother had bought for her, and when she was wearing it, she would pull us on our toboggan through the snow.

Lisa had her own measure of fame. She was featured in a dog calendar for the month of December, had won a silver cup at Crufts dog show in England, and she and I were photographed together in a magazine when I was around eighteen months old. The caption on the photo was "Who's Looking After Whom?" even though it was clear that the dog was the one in charge as I was holding on to the ruff of fur around Lisa's neck in order to remain upright.

Our family dog, Lisa

December 16

The second night was better—up less, more sleep, a bit less biting. But this has to be my last night of sleeping on the couch, because it hurts my back. Tonight, the crate goes into play, even if Fig screams. I've been trying to entice her into it with treats and then leaving the door open but encouraging her to stay there to eat the treat. This is working somewhat, but it will be a whole different thing when I shut the door tonight. Might do it later this afternoon for a trial run, and so I can shower and wash my dishes.

The weird thing about the puppy is that we are strangers, and yet we are locked in an intimate relationship right from the beginning. There is no gradual getting to know each other, and unlike caring for a human baby, there is no genetic link to the infant, never mind being from the same species and thus knowing a little of what that infant needs and feels. So, it's a bond by necessity but does not feel easy. People keep saying to me, "You must be so in love with the puppy." But I'm not. I don't know the puppy, nor the dog she will be, and she doesn't know me either. She would rather be back with her littermates and mother, and I would rather be with a dog that I do know well. I would rather be back with Charlotte.

So, in the absence of feeling, I am depending on routine to cement our bond. I will make a routine that works and I will stick to it, no matter what. Already the constant taking of the puppy out to the yard has made Fig mostly go to the door when she needs to pee, and the switching between bouts of frantic play and naps seems to be working. I just have to stay out of the way of her teeth, which have ripped me and nipped me in a hundred different places. She gets a crazy look in her eyes and just goes for me. It's very hard to dislodge her jaws when they are clamped down over a finger or toe or are tugging at the cuffs of my pants.

I am learning some things about Fig. She is very vocal, cries all the time—in a happy way when she eats, in little grunts when she sleeps, and sometimes just out of what I imagine is loneliness. It must have been so hard to leave behind her wild siblings. I know I am a poor substitute for both mother and littermates. The shock of being removed from one's family must be intense, and however well-meaning I am, nothing I do will be able to match that comfort and familiarity.

Once, I was with my grandfather (my mother's father) in a pub in England, and a couple came in for a drink with their seven yellow Labs. They had bred their dog, and when the six puppies were born, the couple couldn't bear to sell them, so they had simply kept them all. Every evening, they walked them through the village to the pub, where the humans had a drink and the seven large dogs flopped down in a heap under the table, much in the same way as they had probably done for all of their lives together. How confident those dogs must have felt, as their world had never shifted.

Fig and I were up impossibly early this morning, at four thirty. I fed the dog and made coffee, and she had a crazy tear around and then came to sit on the couch with me. She sat by the window and watched the lights of the cars when they passed by, following each one with her eyes until it disappeared down the street. She also watched the snow falling when she went out to pee, lifting her head to watch the drift of the flakes. So many new and wondrous things to discover.

IT WAS READING that made me want to be a writer. I had cried uncontrollably for an entire day after reading *Charlotte's Web* and was so affected by stories—unable to separate them from real life—that I decided the only way to loosen their hold on me would be to create them myself, because then I would know what was coming in the story and wouldn't get so upset.

Of course, I had no idea what being a writer would entail. I was a child when I made that life-directing decision. I often wonder about why we end up doing what we do, if we're lucky enough to be able to choose. It seems so arbitrary. In my case, if I hadn't had a wonderful elementary school teacher who praised my early writing efforts, encouraging me to continue, would I have kept to that path?

In that time and place—the eastern edge of Toronto in the mid-1960s—none of the yards were fenced yet or had grass laid down. There was just a big swath of dirt behind the houses. This was a suburb of new, barely completed houses, populated largely by working-class immigrants from Europe. Many of the neighbourhood dogs wandered freely around this territory, and we got to know them by name and exploit. There was the black Lab up the street called Tero, who had fought with a raccoon and had his tongue split open as a result of the encounter. There was the succession of German shepherds down the

street, all of them called Lucky and each one dying acci-
dentally, way before their time. One "Lucky" was hit by
a car. Another had a seizure, went rigid, and fell down a
flight of stairs.

Life with Lisa was less dramatic, but still intense. The
enormous dog always had ropes of drool hanging down
from her droopy jowls. When she shook her head, the
thick cords of mucus would fly off and stick to the walls
in the house. She instilled anxiety in all of us when she
started to shake her head. There was not much worse
than having one of her snakes of drool drape itself around
your bare arm.

She was fed blocks of horsemeat that were delivered
in a frozen state to the house. They were wrapped in
blue patterned waxed paper, and six of them would
entirely fill the inside of the freezer. Lisa ate half of one
block for every meal. She was fed twice a day, morning
and evening.

Lisa was accepting of other dogs and cats. She let our
household cat sleep in the curl of her tail for warmth in
the winter. I remember her as not so much friendly as just
benignly generous. She put up with things because she
was good-natured. I think now that I must have learned

what *good-natured* meant from watching her example.

She liked swimming and didn't like thunder. She would crawl into bed with my parents or me when there was a storm, panting and anxious, a great 150-pound shaking mess of fear.

When Lisa died of cancer at the age of ten, she was replaced with a dog as small as Lisa was large—Timmy, a long-haired dachshund, weirdly enough the same breed favoured by the Luftwaffe ace who shot down my grandfather's plane in World War II.

My parents had thought that a small dog would be less trouble than a big one, but this was not the case. Timmy barked constantly at any activity on the street, regularly bit people, and urinated or defecated indoors if he was annoyed at something. Once, he lifted his leg on a policeman's polished boot while he stood in our front hall writing out a speeding ticket for my mother.

Ostensibly, Timmy was my dog. My parents gave him to me for Christmas the year I was nine, a year distinguished not only by Lisa's dying but by the magnificent presents I received—perhaps no coincidence. For my birthday I was given a rubber dinghy that had been rowed across Lake Huron by a father and son. There was dried blood on the side of the dinghy from where the father had cut himself on the crossing. I never washed the blood off, and liked to look at it and imagine their voyage while I rowed the dinghy around the more gentle waters of a campground pond.

I went with my mother to fetch Timmy. We had answered an ad in the paper. The little puppy was the runt of the litter and cost twenty-five dollars. He was so small when we brought him home that he could fit inside my father's sheepskin slipper and liked to curl up and sleep in there.

In my *Observer's Book of Dogs*, it stated that dachshunds were a hunting breed, and even though I was not really interested in hunting myself, I had it in my head that Timmy should know how to catch a rabbit or chase a fox. To this end, I spent ages trying to teach him things he wasn't interested in learning. I smeared Marmite all over the yard (we had grass by then) and tried to make him follow a scent. I took him deep into the ravine and tried to coerce him into a fox den, and down to the lake to try and force him to swim.

Many hot summer days were spent traipsing through the raggedy woods near my house, in pursuit of some elusive quarry. I would stamp home afterwards in a bad temper with the exhausted dog trailing behind me on his short, stumpy legs.

Hunting was not remotely what Timmy wanted to be doing. What he liked best was to sit in my father's chair in the living room, barking his head off at any person or dog that happened to walk past the window. He had enemies—people and animals that, for good or bad reason, he had taken against. These included the next-door neighbour, who had kicked him once when he was a puppy and had wandered onto the neighbour's property, and the old man down the end of the street, who had actually done nothing to Timmy, but who, because he was quite old, had an unsteady gait. The dog didn't like the way he walked by the house.

Timmy also didn't like any of the Luckys. If he could get away with it, he liked to attack German shepherds in particular and had once punctured the neck of one at a campground. For a small dog, he was very fierce and completely unafraid of anything bigger than himself—which was most things.

Dogs are sticklers for the way they have learned the world, and they do not easily tolerate change from a routine. They know what they know and they like what they know. This is why, when you get a puppy, you have to expose them to as many different things as possible right away, so the dog will accept them later on. The first few months of a dog's life are very important for their social-ization. Probably Timmy had not met anybody elderly when he was very young, and that was why he had taken against the old man at the end of the street, barking non-stop whenever the man took his slow after-dinner stroll.

Bad dog, good dog—we love them all. I wept over Timmy's body when he died of a heart condition at the age of ten, then drove, sobbing, through the streets in my parents' car in the middle of the night, restless with grief and inconsolable.

After Timmy, my father decided to go back to golden retrievers, the dog of his childhood.

I was nineteen years old and writing seriously all the time, spurred on by the odd poem being published in the odd little magazine, but I was unsure how to go about making my life as a writer. Should I go to university and study English, which would allow me to keep reading and perhaps give me access to other like-minded people? Or should I just work at whatever job I could get, because this would give me experiences, which I knew were important in terms of giving me something to write about?

I only knew one writer, a friend of a friend's father. He had hit a low spot in his own publishing career, and rather than give me the optimistic encouragement I craved, he used to take me out for a beer and complain about his agent and lack of readership.

I was writing mostly poetry and using it as a way to work out my strong teenage feelings. Poetry lends itself to emotional firsts, and the voice-driven nature of it was intoxicating to me at the time. When I wasn't writing my own poetry, I was reading Dylan Thomas and T.S. Eliot, Elizabeth Bishop and W.H. Auden.

After being suspended from regular high school for an assortment of authority-defying behaviours, I attended an alternative school, where I accelerated my studies and completed my education a full term ahead of everyone else. The emphasis on independent study at the alternative school suited me, as I had struggled with, and rebelled against, the confines of traditional education. By finishing high school early, I had eight months to work at a job to earn money for university. It seemed a good plan, especially as I had been accepted into my first choice of university and English program. I was excited about school again after my success at the alternative school.

This was the early 1980s. There was a recession and high unemployment in Canada. Jobs were hard to come by and there wasn't a lot of choice. I felt lucky to land work at a full-service car wash in downtown Toronto, where I laboured for eleven and a half hours a day without scheduled breaks. My job was to stand in the car wash tunnel by the rinse arch and hop into the car being shunted along the track. Once inside, I would spray the windows with cleaner, wipe them down as well as the dashboard, replace the floor mats and drive the car out to the front, where I would pass it over to be hand-dried, and sprint back up the tunnel to hop into the next car. On a busy day we would wash 750 cars and I was constantly in motion.

I had nothing in common with my fellow workers, most of whom were older men, but I made friends nonetheless, bonding over the physicality of the job and the surprising things that happened at the car wash. Once, someone brought a gun to work. Another time, two men were sent to paint the roof and fell asleep up there. We had to stand in the parking lot and throw pebbles at them to try to wake them up before they rolled off the edge. Sometimes a car would be left in drive and, pushed along by the rollers in the tunnel, would pick up speed and come hurtling out the chute like a bull at a rodeo. Our only method of stopping it was to drop the industrial door at the end of the tunnel and watch the car plow through it, scattering glass and metal everywhere, and hopefully be slowed down enough so the runaway car wouldn't continue onto Front Street and cause a traffic accident.

Thoughts of school receded in the wake of what I thought of as "real life" at the car wash. My friends who were finishing their last term of high school seemed immature when compared to my best friend at the car wash, an alcoholic in his fifties named Bill, who had once worked on the lake freighters.

My family was an artistic one. My mother played the piano very well and had her ARCT qualifications. My father was an ardent opera lover with a huge record collection. He listened to music for hours every night, after working at his accountancy business during the day. The bass from his stereo was so loud it shook my bedroom floor, but I learned to sleep through it. My brother, Martin, was a musical prodigy and practised eight hours a day, having started playing the piano at the age of four. My sister, Cathy, was learning sculpture. So, there was no objection from anyone to my wanting to be a writer, although my father warned me that it might be a hard way to make a living and that I should probably have a backup plan.

My parents did not have strong opinions about my attending university, and the idea of going disappeared in the tide of excitement and immediacy at the car wash. So, I never took my place at the English program I'd been accepted into.

December 17

Last night, I put the crate right up onto my bed and Fig slept in it without too much fuss. It went better than expected. We were up twice in the night, but I didn't let her out for good in the morning until it was my regular getting-up time. Sleep, though interrupted, had at least happened.

After her breakfast, during which I managed to wash about half of my stack of dishes, which had been piling up for four days, I put on her little harness and fleece jacket and put her into the passenger seat of the car, with the seat warmer on. We drove to pick up our walking friend and went to our usual walking spot at the conservation area. Because the puppy can't really go on the ground until after her second set of shots, we made a sling out of a blanket and I carried her through the park. It was a snowy but sunny morning, and the world was very beautiful. We saw a barred owl and a Cooper's hawk, and several people stopped to pat the dog's little head, poking out from her blanket sling.

There was a strange moment as we were crossing the big field where just months ago Charlotte had walked ahead of us. I had had a similar moment a few weeks ago, when I gave a reading in a place where my brother had once played a concert. I stood on stage just a few feet away from the piano he had played there, maybe fifteen years before, well before he died. I thought about it afterwards, how it wasn't so much a memory as an intersection—the two events came together in the same place and touched one another. It felt like that this morning, with the new puppy in my arms, walking along the path in winter that Charlotte had trotted along in summer. The events were touching but were separated from each other by time.

WORKING AT THE CAR WASH was exhausting, and while the experience was exhilarating, I wasn't getting a lot of writing done. When I wasn't running up and down the car wash tunnel, I was eating or sleeping, occasionally reading. The job took most of my energy. I couldn't afford to wander through Europe, as the dead writers I admired had once done, but I did sense that I needed to go somewhere to write and see if I really had what it took to work at words all day every day.

At the age of twenty, I went to live in England with my grandmother.

My father's mother was a war widow. The grandfather I never met was shot down over the Mediterranean in 1941. She lived alone in the house my father had grown up in, on the edge of the Ashdown Forest in the south of England. A lifelong dog lover, she had once bred golden retrievers and had four dogs when she met and married my grandfather. When my parents were courting, she had a dog named Wendy, who liked to collect golf balls from the nearby golf course. She would fit as many as she could inside her mouth to carry home. My grandmother had a jar in the hall where she put the golf balls, returning them to the golf course when the jar became full.

The first time my family went back to England after the emigration, we went to my grandmother's house for a visit. I was five years old and my brother was two. He was allowed in the house at tea time because he was still so close to being a baby, but I, being older, was left outside in the charge of my grandmother's golden retriever Kirsty. (My grandmother thought young children were a nuisance and didn't want them indoors.) The dog was to keep me from wandering out onto the road—which she did—and to make sure I didn't get into any trouble—which she was less good at. For a while, we stood companionably together in the garage, and then I lumbered out into the front garden with the dog right behind me. She blocked me with her body from going too far away from the house, but she didn't stop me from picking all the leaves of my grandmother's lamb's ears and posting them through the letter box.

It was my mother's idea that I go to live with my grandmother, to help her out in her big Sussex house and make sure she didn't have a fall. In return, I would have a free place to live and write for a year. It wasn't Hemingway's Paris, but it was the best option available to me, so I went.

Going back to England was a return, not just to my childhood, but also to my father's. I slept in the room where he had slept, in the bed that had once been his. The room was at the back of the house, with windows that overlooked the garden. There was a circular rose bed and a small orchard. I would open the casement window and smoke, dangling over the sill and staring out to the row of yews and mounds of composting leaves at the back edge of the half-acre lawn.

In a cupboard in one of the many empty bedrooms were my grandfather's spare RAF uniform and his flight logbooks. The brass buttons on the jacket were still shiny, and the trousers still carried a crease, forty years on.

There was a coal cellar, accessed through a small metal door round the side of the house, and inside was a huge load of coal from the war. My grandmother hadn't lit a coal fire since her husband had died, preferring to use an electric fire in the sitting room instead of the fireplace in the dining room. The winter I was there, I made a fire every day and burned through the entire cellar of World War II coal.

My grandmother and I were together out of necessity and mostly avoided each other. She wasn't a very warm or friendly person, and I didn't know her well. The house was large. I kept to one side of it and my grandmother kept to the other. We ate breakfast and lunch separately, but met, briefly, for supper every night—a boiled egg and toast, or potted meat on toast and an apple or pear—which I prepared and pushed on a gold tin trolley to her side of the house. We ate in matching wingback armchairs in front of her electric fire. There was never much conversation, but our silence wasn't uncomfortable. It amused my grandmother that I was writing a novel, but we never really talked about it. Once, during supper, my grandmother told me that she was thinking of killing herself when she turned eighty.

"I'm just going to take some pills and be done with it," she said. "Eighty is long enough to live."

She was seventy-eight at that point. Like much of what she said, her intention to commit suicide was uttered very flatly, with no feeling, so it was easy to ignore. My grandmother stated it as matter-of-factly as though she was asking me to pass the butter.

She had no dogs at the time, having given up her beloved golden retrievers when she was in her sixties and could no longer walk the distances necessary to exercise them. Some of her desire to die could have come from the loneliness she felt at no longer having any canine companions. She had lived with dogs her entire life—first the family dogs, and then owning and caring for her first golden retriever when she was just eleven. She still had paintings and photographs of her dogs throughout the house.

My grandmother's road housed several retired military officers, including famous Colonel Maurice Buckmaster, who had trained spies for British Special Operations during the war. He was made an Officer of the Order of the British Empire and had a portrait of himself hanging over his sitting room fireplace. He also had a small barky terrier, as did the retired major next door to my grandmother. Neither dog helped assuage our collective nostalgia for our family pets. "Yappy little things," my grandmother said of the terriers. "I always want to step on them."

I had decided to write a novel while at my grandmother's house, because I felt I should write hard every day, to see if I had the discipline for it. Poetry, my usual form, couldn't be harnessed in the way prose could. My poems were often written quickly, in a rush of words and feeling, and it would be impossible to work all day at them the way I anticipated working on a novel. But my book progressed slowly. Writing all day was hard, although not as hard as the loneliness that attended it. (A fact that I have found to be true all through my subsequent writing life.)

I worked at one end of a massive walnut table in the dining room, with my back to the garden windows for the light. At the other end of the room was the coal fire and a huge portrait in oils of my father as a child. Whenever I looked up from the page, I saw him there, aged about six and wearing a sort of pink jumpsuit, painted in the act of climbing down from the bench where he'd been made to sit by the artist. It was strange to see him as a child, and I admired his disobedience in the painting. (He had been, my grandmother said, "a difficult child.")

When I think now of living in my grandmother's house and working on my novel, I find it hard to remember the writing part, even though I was actively writing for the majority of my hours there. But writing is largely an internal process. It relies on the thoughts and feelings of the moment, and I no longer have access to those thoughts and feelings, having moved so far past them and not being someone who has ever kept a journal. But I do remember the feeling of writing itself from those days, which was largely a feeling of loneliness, shot through sometimes with a jolt of excitement when the words and phrases came out in a surprising and pleasing order.

I would write at my makeshift desk from nine in the morning until one, when I would break for lunch. In the afternoons, I would walk in the countryside or do errands for my grandmother in the village, and then return to writing in the hours before supper. In the evenings, I read by the coal fire. There were no books in my grandmother's house, but there was a small library in the village hall, where I went every week to borrow some.

At the ages of twenty and twenty-one, I only had the company of one elderly and fairly misanthropic person. I saw my cousins sometimes, but mostly I was without the company of anyone my age, and I was still too shy to seek out strangers. But perhaps that was what was required for me to be a writer. Perhaps other writers can work with family around, with people coming and going, with constant interruption. But I have never been that kind of writer. In order to open myself to the thoughts and feelings that are necessary to the work, I have had to turn away from people. Over the years, I have grown used to this and don't mind it as I used to, but in my formative years as a writer, it was very hard to reconcile myself to it. I was excruciatingly lonely during those years in England, craving the company of people my age, and I can still feel the sting of it when I think back.

Because I hadn't gone to university, I depended on reading for my education, and I read widely and voraciously. Before I went to Britain, I had devoured Sylvia Plath's *The Bell Jar* and *Ariel*. I especially loved the poetry, with its sharpness and candour, and so, when Plath's *Collected Poems* were first published, I skipped writing for the day and made the one-hour train journey to London to buy a copy.

I read the poems slowly and often out loud, saying the words over and over again, like a spell, to ward off the four p.m. darkness, the winter, the acute loneliness. I came to know the poems intimately. The words drilled their way into my brain, and even now, I can quote large sections of them from memory.

I finished Plath's book and my own. My grandmother turned eighty and did not kill herself. I returned to Canada, proud of myself for having finished my novel and resolute in my decision to be a writer. It didn't matter that the novel was bad and I knew it. The quality of the work had never been the point of my time in England. I had proven to myself that I had what it took to write every day, and I was determined to keep that newly made space open. I worked one lousy job after another, but I wrote hard and published—first poetry, then eventually novels. In my thirties, I applied and was accepted into the arts colony Yaddo in Saratoga Springs, New York.

When I arrived, I couldn't believe my luck in being given the studio that Sylvia Plath had used when she had been there forty years before; a third-floor room in West House with skylights, set amidst the tops of the pine trees. (Yaddo had ten thousand hundred-year-old pine trees and was always very dark. There were sometimes bats out during the daylight hours.)

At Yaddo, there was a library with books from all the people who had been resident there, so it was easy to access Sylvia Plath's published journal and read the entries for her 1959 stay. She described her writer's studio in detail, and I was thrilled to discover that nothing had changed in that room from her time to mine. The furniture was not only the same furniture but was positioned where it had always been—wooden table by the window, single iron bedstead against the sloping attic wall.

I don't remember what I wrote while I was in that studio, but I do remember the feel of the room, how it was cheerful, and how I liked being there, climbing the narrow stairs to it every morning with my provided lunch box in hand.

While at Yaddo, I kept a detailed food diary, noting that residents were divided about the merits of the meatloaf sandwich, and putting an asterisk beside the best dinner—homemade salmon cakes, served with wild rice and asparagus.

Years have passed. I have kept on with my writing life, following roughly the same habits I put in place for myself when I was twenty and living in England, only now I have the company of a dog during my working day.

Last Christmas, a friend gave me the newly published second volume of Sylvia Plath's letters. It is over a thousand pages long and I swear that the bookmark never moves, that the unread portion of the book grows larger every day. Multiple times I have felt like giving up—not because I have lost interest in reading the letters, but because the minutiae of Sylvia Plath's life has begun taking up too much space in my own head. I have gone to sleep thinking about her and woken up thinking about her. It has felt like a kind of madness, the way falling in love feels.

When I was twenty, Sylvia Plath dying at thirty didn't seem young to me. In fact, it seemed quite old. Now that I am almost sixty, thirty seems impossibly young, and reading of Plath's increasingly desperate struggle to manage her life in those last terrible months is heartbreaking because I know how it ends. We all know how it ends.

The quantity of domestic detail makes reading the letters a weird experience. Sylvia Plath is essentially a stranger, and yet after a month of reading her letters, I now know more about her daily life than I know about anyone else's daily life. I find myself caring that she gets her washing machine to help with the endless labour of Court Green, her Devon house. I am outraged on her behalf that the house is so cold she gets chilblains, and touched by her baking a carrot cake for the midwives who attend the birth of her children. In fact, the letters feel so intimate, so close, that it almost seems as though I could slip into her life from the future and give her the help she repeatedly asked for during the unbearably cold and bleak winter of 1963.

Plath was the age of my mother. I was the age of her children. Much of what was in her life is recognizable from mine. There is a lot of slippage between our two worlds.

One evening when I was at Yaddo, there was a performance by a composer in the drawing room of West House. It was a regular thing for residents to play their music or read their poetry to the other assembled artists. Plath and Ted Hughes both gave readings when they were there in the fall of 1959.

This particular evening, the sun was going down and the room in West House glowed with a golden light, enhanced by the gold curtains and gold velvet chairs. The composer began to play the piano, and as I listened, I thought of all the other musicians who had sat at that piano in this elegant drawing room, year after year after year, and how the furnishings were the constant thing and the people were like ghosts, appearing and then vanishing, each individual, but also successive and continuous.

Five years later, when I was at Yaddo again, I stayed in East House, which was where the administrator for the colony in Plath's time, Elizabeth Ames, had lived and died. (She is buried on the property.) Those of us who lived in her house during the April I was there used her dishes and played her records in the evening, sat on her couch and walked over her Persian rugs. We were her guests and yet not her guests.

Although we are in our own particular bodies, having our own experiences, we are also constantly sliding in and out of time, some of it not belonging to us at all. This is how I briefly slipped into Sylvia Plath's world, and how I inhabited parts of my father's childhood in England during my time in my grandmother's house.

My grandmother is long dead. Her house, which she lived in for over sixty years, was sold after her death and renovated by the new owners. I found the listing online a few months ago, when it was being sold again, and I looked through the twenty-six photos of the house and garden.

The rooms downstairs have all been reconfigured into one open-plan layout. Gone is the poky kitchen and the dining room where I had once written an excruciatingly bad novel. Unsurprisingly, the coal fireplace has been removed entirely. All the dark oak floors have been replaced with light-coloured hardwood. The casement windows have given way to French doors that open onto a blank, green lawn. My grandmother's circular rose garden, once the focal point of the backyard, has been completely grassed over. The orchard is gone, and the conservatory from what I still think of as her side of the house. In fact, the whole house, except for the iron-studded oak front door, is unrecognizable.

But this is what I wonder: if sometimes the people who lived there after my grandmother, and the people who will live there after them, walking through the new, massive kitchen and dining area, found themselves thinking of a word or a phrase, saying it out loud perhaps. A word like *heart* or *star* or *breath*, one of the words that I shook out from that blue book of charms, from Sylvia Plath's *Collected Poems*, all those years ago, and which might still float around that space, even though the space has become so changed. And I wonder if there is ever a mysterious scent of apples in the autumn on the bare strip of grass where the orchard used to stand, or if sometimes the new occupants wake to the barking of a dog, and when they rise and go to the window, there is nothing out there.

A beloved aunt of mine died this winter. She had lived in England, along with all of my extended family, but I saw her many times over the years and was close to her. When people die, they sometimes return briefly in a triumphant way via dreams or memories, as though we are trying to fix them in our firmament in the most optimal position. My aunt comes back to me as middle-aged, striding out over the Wentworth golf course near her home in Surrey, her dog bounding ahead through the bracken. My aunt's favourite dog was a pure white collie named Shadow. A funny name, given the colour of the dog, but he was named for his habit of being quietly alongside my aunt through every moment of the day, pressed next to her like her own shadow. It is easy to bring back the dead by thinking of their dogs. There is something always alive in the memory of a dog.

My grandmother is dead, as is my father. I don't live in the country I was born in, and sometimes I long for it, for the family there and the life that might have been mine, if we had stayed.

Shortly after my grandmother died, I was visiting my parents' house, sitting in the living room with my father. It was dark out, but neither of us had turned on a light or pulled the curtains over the large picture window.

"Well," said my father in the half gloom, "my mother is dead. Next it will be me, and then, I'm afraid, it will be you."

I don't remember what I said back to him, something along the lines of "That's still a long way off yet," but I do remember his words exactly, and think of them often. Because, of course, what was once a long way away isn't a long way off anymore. My father is now dead too, and I am suddenly at the front of the queue.

I don't know what my life would have been like if we had remained in the UK, but I like to wonder on it sometimes. Mostly what I imagine are family occasions such as Christmas, and I think how it would have been to feel a solid part of the large family we left behind—grandparents, aunts and uncles, cousins—how good it would feel to be in a room filled with all of them, and how rarely that has happened in my life.

I also think about dogs when I imagine the life of staying rather than leaving. I think about how dogs are allowed in pubs and some restaurants, on trains, in hotels, and about all the good and glorious places in the British countryside to walk a dog. I think about how the British people often lavish more love on their dogs than they do on their spouses or children. My father too showed more physical affection to his golden retrievers than he did to his children, but I don't remember that we really minded very much. It seemed perfectly reasonable to have the dog at the top of that particular hierarchy.

All of my cousins have dogs, and from their postings on social media, it looks like their dogs are held in the same high regard as my father's were, and as are my own. Whenever I visit with these cousins—infrequently now that we are older and entrenched in our separate lives—we can always immediately reconnect by asking about the dogs. It is through our dogs that we remember who we are to one another—that we still somehow belong together.

CHARACTER

CHARACTER

December 18

It turns out that I wasn't screaming loud enough to stop Fig from biting me. "Bite inhibition" requires shrieks of murderous proportions, and when the vocal pitch is agonizingly shrill, only then will the puppy unhook her razor teeth from my flesh.

I woke to temperatures of minus twenty-six, so there is no possibility of taking the puppy outside. It was hard to even get her to go out for a pee. Every time I took her out and set her down in the snow, she ran back up the steps to the house to try and return to the warmth. So, we went for a drive instead, with the heated front seats on and piles of blankets. I fed her lots of treats in the car, so she will like it there, but she already seems very relaxed by car travel and mostly sleeps in her little blanket cocoon.

There's a change today, in both of us. We like one another more. She is napping on top of me, sometimes curling herself around my neck like a cat, and we are looking at each other more, making eye contact. I know that this is one of the ways that dogs bond, one of the ways they show you that they are connected, by making eye contact, so I am glad of the changes. Also, I am not worrying so much about the constant work of having the puppy keeping me from doing much else, but rather I'm just going with it and scraping out ten minutes here and there to tidy the kitchen or move the laundry back upstairs.

I enrolled the puppy in kindergarten, which starts after the holidays, in January, and I learned, through their literature, that a puppy should meet a hundred different people before they are three months old. I have to step up my game! Next week, I will take the puppy into some of the big box stores, which are sure to be busy during this pre-Christmas period and where we could probably meet a hundred different people in a single day.

Today, I was thinking that it doesn't really matter that

Charlotte was the dog of my life, in that everything is a continuum—love, writing, dogs. My grandmother, after my grandfather's disappearance over the Mediterranean, gave up on life, gave up her hobbies and interests, never dated or married again. She was just thirty-five! Perhaps my grandfather was her great love, but she probably could have loved again, if she had chosen that.

Human loves are not all equal, and neither is the love we have for our dogs. Writing too is not all the same. Some work is simply better than others, or we are more connected to the material, so it feels more true. But the important thing is that we engage with it all, and in the engagement is life and attachment to life. It doesn't matter that everything isn't equal. It's simplistic to believe that after a great love there is no other.

I took the puppy to the vet to get her checked over. There were many squeals over her cuteness from the desk staff. She tried to eat the vet's stethoscope while her heart rate was being measured—it was 180, which seemed impossibly high to me, but I was assured that it was within the normal range for a puppy. (No wonder dogs die well before we do, if they are using their hearts up like that.)

Friends came by. Fig went uncomplainingly into her crate for a couple of hours so I could answer emails. Another friend came and watched her for an hour so I could go and do some grocery shopping. (The standard for crating a puppy is one hour for every month of age—so two hours maximum for Fig. To keep the crate a relatively positive experience, I don't want to crate her too many times during a day.) Tonight, more friends are coming over and I will make a fire, which always made Charlotte very soporific, and I'm hopeful for the same effect on the puppy.

I'm getting a glimpse of who Fig is. She is a bit wary of things and people but always moves towards them, never away from them. She tries and fails at climbing the back steps, and then keeps trying until she masters the three steps up from the yard to the back door. Then she takes that lesson and applies it to the stairs between the first and second floor, racing up all thirteen of them with impressive speed in a kind of showing-off way while friends put on their coats in the hall. She has spirit. The vet today called her "sparky."

Right now, as I type this, she is passed out on the couch by my legs, snoring loudly. The snout of the vizsla grows as they mature, but when they are born, they have squashed-in faces and look a bit like little furry pigs. Puppies often snore because of the compressed muzzle. When their noses grow as they age into dogs, their breathing becomes less noisy.

Before I brought the puppy home, I had a fantasy that while Fig dozed beside me, I would read all the books that teeter in piles around my office, bought sometimes years ago and still unread. I thought I would be able to draw and write copious notes for this book; that I would talk on the phone with friends, or write lengthy letters. I had the fantasy that my isolation with the dog would be a kind of leisure period.

But the reality is, of course, different than that. First, the puppy doesn't doze for long, so there is only time to bang out a few sentences here, or answer an email, and then she's awake and tearing around again, trying to draw blood with her mouth full of tiny knives. Also, she is often sleeping on me or across me, making it impossible to draw or write or read. Any tiny movement wakes her up, as do voices, so talking on the phone is also out.

What does work is people coming to the house, and I am seeing more of my friends and family than usual, and just have to take that as a gift and forget about the fanciful idea of tearing through book after book while a contented and calm puppy naps beside me.

The biting frenzy is worse in the mornings. Something about being cooped up all night in the crate, I guess. I have so many puncture wounds on my hands that they have become stiff with bruising. Fig also sliced through my lip and bit hard on my cheekbone. I look like I have been in a fist fight. Bite inhibition is going to take ages, I fear.

She's more confident now, more sure of her surroundings and her place in them. She likes to crawl under the couch and under the dining room table, has started hoarding her toys under the table, making it her den.

In my hour of freedom today, I had a shower and washed my hair, then cleaned the kitchen and ate lunch. It felt incredible. To think that, just a week ago, I could do whatever I wanted with my time!

BECAUSE I DIDN'T GO to university and relied on reading for my education, I decided on a systematic process. I started at *A* in the literature section of the local library and I read everything in that section, moving slowly forward through the alphabet. It took a long time to get to the letter *M* and, growing impatient with my methodical approach, I skipped ahead to *W* so that I could read Virginia Woolf.

I read Woolf for years—all the novels, which I found a bit formal for my tastes, and the volumes of letters and diaries, which I enjoyed much more. I followed Woolf's example of how to live a writing day—working in the morning, walking in the afternoon, writing letters or listening to music in the evenings. That was the template I was working from when I was trying to be a writer in England in my early twenties, and I've always found it to be a good fit for my writing life.

Virginia Woolf lived in the countryside of East Sussex, in the same general area as my family, both sides of which are from the towns and villages of the High Weald, an Area of Outstanding Natural Beauty that was once the most wooded area of Britain.

There are many photographs of Virginia Woolf in books and online, but I decide to go looking for photographs of her dogs and find one of Grizzle in the Harvard University Archives. In the photograph, the dog is leaning over the wall in front of Monk's House, the English country property of Virginia and Leonard Woolf in Rodmell, Sussex.

Grizzle was a mongrel terrier of medium size. In the photograph, she has her elbows on the top of the stone wall and is angling her body towards the photographer, who is Virginia Woolf. The expression in the dog's eyes is one I saw many times on the face of my dog Charlotte. It is a combination of *What are you doing?* and *I didn't say you could do that.* It is a bit concerned and a bit proprietary, and it tells me more about Virginia Woolf than any photograph I have seen of the author herself, because it shows her in direct, real-time relation to her dog. A dog is always candid, always honest, and so the look in Grizzle's eyes is an honest assessment of the type of relationship that Woolf had with her dog, and shows us, the viewer, how the dog cared for and took care of Woolf.

Woolf had Grizzle from 1919 to near the end of 1926, when the dog had to be euthanized because she developed mange and then fits. She was preceded and replaced by a spaniel, but Woolf had a special fondness for Grizzle, whom she had adopted as an adult dog from the Battersea Dogs Home, an animal shelter that has been in existence in the UK since 1860. Grizzle accompanied the author on her daily walks over the South Downs and was such a presence in Woolf's life that she features in a famous diary passage about the soul: "And the truth is, one can't write directly about the soul. Looked at, it vanishes: but look at the ceiling, at Grizzle, at the cheaper beasts in the Zoo which are exposed to walkers in Regents Park, & the soul slips in."[1]

Dogs were a presence in Virginia Woolf's life right from the beginning, and they continued to be right to the end. She believed that dogs represented "the private side of life—the play side."[2] But dogs, like friends or lovers, do not all occupy a similar place in one's life, nor do they evoke similar feelings. Some dogs we tend to love more than others, and some dogs come into our lives during happier times than other dogs do. Grizzle came into Woolf's life at a good moment. She was thirty-seven when she acquired the dog, and forty-four when Grizzle had to be euthanized. These were potent years for the writer. She was in the prime of her life, the rich middle of it. Books were written, energy was high, and during this period, Woolf embarked on a dynamic affair with the writer and aristocrat Vita Sackville-West, which resulted in the book *Orlando*, one of her most ebullient and imaginative works.

Grizzle is sometimes conflated with Woolf in her letters to Sackville-West. On April 13, 1926, Woolf wrote to Sackville-West, "Remember your dog Grizzle and your Virginia, waiting you; both rather mangy; but what of that? These shabby mongrels are always the most loving, warm-hearted creatures. Grizzle and Virginia will rush down to meet you—they will lick you all over."[3]

A few months later, when she was feeling less loving towards Vita, Virginia wrote to her:

That's what comes of attacking your poor Virginia and dog Grizzle. They bite instantly.

But at the same time they adore; and if you hadn't the eyes of a newt and the blood of a toad, you'd see it, and not need telling. . . . [4]

How integral a dog becomes to the life and work of their person says something about the importance of that dog to that person. Grizzle was there in the midst of Woolf's love affair with Sackville-West. She was there as the model for a dog called Gipsy in Woolf's 1940 short story "Gipsy, the Mongrel." By now, the real Grizzle was dead, so the story serves as a memorial to Woolf's canine friend. It's a simple story—one couple telling another couple a story about their former dog. In a sly nod to Woolf's dog, the man telling the story is described as having "a little griz-zled moustache over his upper teeth. . . ."[5] The dog herself is described as having "a coat as rough as a door scraper."[6] It is not the dog's looks that are her draw, but rather her charm and personality. The narrator of the story calls her "a dog of remarkable character."[7]

This character showed itself in her barking at the ring-ing phone, and stamping out matches for lit cigarettes with her paws. (Woolf taught all of her subsequent dogs to put out the matches for her cigarettes.) It also showed in the dog passing judgment on any guests to the house. She licked the hands of the guests whom she liked and wished to stay. The visitors whom she didn't care for, she indicated her dislike of them by rushing to the door when they were there, to show them that they should leave. According to the narrator of the story, she never made a mistake in that regard and was a very good judge of char-acter. She is described as being "a dog of sense."[8]

It would be hard not to find a dog charming that passed judgment on visitors and perhaps did what the host could never do, in trying to usher them out the door. Are our best dogs, our favourite dogs, the ones who do the things that we cannot bring ourselves to do? Do they do it for us? Certainly, the look that Grizzle has in her photograph is the look of a confident dog, one who would have no qualms about telling someone to leave her house.

"Dogs can't talk," Virginia Woolf says in her little story about "Gipsy," but "dogs remember."[9] So, a dog will remember whom they like and whom they don't, and what is in one person's character to admire and what is in another's to despise.

The little story ends with the dog running from the house, probably to die, on December 16, which was the day that the real Grizzle died. She was taken to be euthanized by Leonard Woolf when Virginia was visiting Vita Sackville-West; so to all intents and purposes, the real dog did just disappear, as the fictional dog does, and perhaps, as the narrator of the story wonders, Virginia Woolf felt that Grizzle was still out there somewhere, that she hadn't really died, but simply vanished into the darkness.

Grizzle gets a final mention in the last pages of *Orlando*, in a passage about the meaning of life: "Here she was in St. James's Street; a married woman; with a ring on her finger; where there had been a coffee house once there was now a restaurant; it was about half past three in the afternoon; the sun was shining; there were three pigeons;

a mongrel terrier dog; two hansom cabs and a barouche landau. What then, was Life?"[10]

Life for Woolf was a morning of writing and an afternoon of walking with a dog, a routine she maintained for most of her life, and which I have followed for most of mine.

The Woolfs' house at Rodmell, Monk's House, first opened to the public in 1982. Virginia Woolf had died in 1941, and Leonard Woolf in 1969. Various tenants and caretakers had lived in the house since then, but when it

Grizzle, in a photograph taken by Virginia Woolf

was opened to the public by the National Trust in 1982, there was still much in the house that had belonged to the Woolfs and it was much less "curated" than it is today. There was still the sense of it being a home rather than a display.

I was twenty-one and living in England in 1982, and I made a pilgrimage to Monk's House in the month that it opened, walking a portion of the way there from where I was living near East Grinstead.

The decoration by Vanessa Bell and Duncan Grant on much of the furniture and fabrics was impressive, so too the sunken aspect to the living room and its pale green paint—a shade chosen by Virginia Woolf herself. But the single thing that made me feel the presence of Virginia Woolf in the house, above anything else, were the old dog leads hanging on a hook by the back door.

BEING WITH ANY YOUNG ANIMAL (and I include babies in this) is an excellent way to study character. How does anyone become who they are? What are the subtle shifts of personality growth? One of the reasons I like having a dog from puppyhood is because I will be there for all of their development and will know the dog deeply. There will be no surprises. I will not have to piece together my dog's backstory based on individual bits of evidence that present themselves over time.

My parents once had a golden retriever who had been a rescue. He was afraid of the basement and the kitchen. It took ages for them to figure out that he wasn't actually scared of the rooms themselves, but rather the concrete of the basement floor and the linoleum on the kitchen floor—surfaces where he had likely once been punished. My mother put a carpet runner across the middle of the kitchen floor, so he would feel okay about being in the room, but he was always uneasy making the passage across it to the back door.

What I have learned from my dogs about character is that there can be anomalies in a personality. A brave dog can be afraid of thunder. A gentle dog can take a sudden dislike to someone and not be convinced out of it. Human beings and dogs are not perfect equations where everything makes sense. There is often incongruity in character, and sometimes this is the most interesting part of someone. When writing characters, it is okay to create something in them that is a bit of a wild card. In my novel *The Lost Garden*, I have a World War II soldier who knits—a small thing perhaps, but a character anomaly on which a large part of the story turns.

There are certain things you can do to influence a dog's behaviour. Consistency and calmness help to give dogs confidence and to allow them to not have to be hyper-vigilant. But behaviour is different from character. The former can be modified, the latter is fairly fixed and has to be borne. But once you learn someone's character, you can figure out how to work around it. Character can be mitigated by attachment. The greater one's attachment to another, the more one will forgive. And nowhere is this better displayed than in one's relationship to dogs. Character traits that would be judged to be intolerable in a fellow human being are often tolerated in a dog.

Thomas Hardy had a fox terrier named Wessex, who was so territorial that he regularly attacked guests to the Hardys' home, often ripping their trouser legs. He also walked on the tabletop during dinner, helping himself to whatever morsel of food he fancied from people's plates. The local postman, trying to defend himself from one of the dog's ferocious attacks, kicked out two of his front teeth.

Thomas Hardy with Wessex

Wessex was originally purchased by Hardy's wife, Florence, to be a guard dog at their home in Dorchester, and he took his job very seriously. The servants lived in fear of him, and he regularly bit people, including the author John Galsworthy. Wessex had a terrible temper, and even the simplest of trespasses against him, such as clipping his coat, required Herculean efforts. Florence described him during one clipping session as "bursting with rage."

One thing that Wessex did like was the radio. His favourite program was *Children's Hour*, and Thomas Hardy bought him his own radio, which Wessex would sit in front of, dutifully listening. If they were out when it was time for *Children's Hour*, Wessex would cry to be taken home so he wouldn't miss the program.

When he died, at the age of thirteen, Hardy was heartbroken and wrote several poems about Wessex, including one from the dog's point of view, "Dead 'Wessex' the Dog to the Household," which ends with these lines:

Should you call as when I knew you,
Wistful ones,
Should you call as when I knew you,
Shared your home;
Should you call as when I knew you,
I shall not turn to view you,
I shall not listen to you,
Shall not come.

Wessex was a difficult dog, but an impressive and memorable character. My dogs have all had strong characters, and I have learned from them that to have traits that are admirable is as good as having traits that are likeable. When I create a character in a novel, I am mindful of this. In my novel *The Reinvention of Love*, the character of Charles Sainte-Beuve is not particularly likeable, but he has two traits that make him sympathetic: humour and devotion—both very dog-like traits, come to think of it.

Character, in dogs, often comes in challenging form. But is there something in the chaos of a difficult character that stirs the imagination of a writer, that freshens it? Can a bad dog help to make a good writer?

E.B. White, the author of the famous children's book *Charlotte's Web*, which I had ardently wept over when young, had a number of dogs over his lifetime—mostly dachshunds—and wrote wonderfully about the human-dog relationship.

The dog he documented the most (even continuing to write about the dog after he had died) was his dachshund Fred, who accompanied White on his farm duties in an overseeing capacity. He was not an easy dog, and indeed did not even seem to like White very much, except in an opportunistic way. White wrote:

Fred devoted his life to deflating me and succeeded admirably. His attachment to our establishment, though untinged with affection, was strong nevertheless, and vibrant. It was simply that he found in our persons, in our activities, the sort of complex, disorderly society that fired his imagination and satisfied his need for tumult and his quest for truth.[11]

White noted that some dogs are so monumental that they do not disappear, even after they have died. He continued to invoke the character of Fred in various essays and letters, and he would go down to the scrubby woodland where Fred was buried and keep

E.B. White and one of his dachshunds, Minnie

an eye on what was happening there, the way that Fred had kept an eye on the place when he was alive. It was the only grave that White ever visited, and he went often.

The writer and illustrator James Thurber always had dogs, sometimes as many as fourteen at a time. He drew them and wrote about them and constantly featured them in the cartoons he published in *The New Yorker*. He loved living with them and believed that dogs represent balance and serenity, and are "a sound creature in a crazy world."

The most infamous of his dogs was one he had in childhood, Muggs, an Airedale terrier who regularly bit people—not just visitors to the home but most members of the household as well. Thurber's mother, who maintained that the dog always felt sorry afterwards, made it a habit to send each person who had been attacked by Muggs a box of candy at Christmas. At one point, she was sending out upwards of forty boxes of candy each yuletide. Thurber immortalized Muggs in an aptly named story, "The Dog Who Bit People." The following passage is taken from this story:

Lots of people reported our Airedale to the police but my father held a municipal office at the time and was on friendly terms with the police. Even so, the cops had been out a couple of times—once when Muggs bit Mrs. Rufus Sturtevant and again when he bit Lieutenant-Governor Malloy—but mother told them that it hadn't been Muggs' fault but the fault of the people who had been bitten. "When he starts for them, they scream," she explained, "and that excites him." The cops suggested that it might be a good idea to tie the dog up, but mother said that it mortified him to be tied up and that he wouldn't eat when he was tied up.

Muggs ferociously attacked anyone who set his dish of food on the floor, so Mrs. Thurber put his food on an old kitchen table and he sat on a bench to eat it. The dog spent most of his time outdoors, and the only thing he was afraid of was thunderstorms, and when he heard the sound of thunder, he would bolt for the house. So, Mrs. Thurber devised a contraption out of a length of sheet iron with a wooden handle that she could shake to imitate the sound of thunder, and that was her way of calling Muggs home.

Dogs, after the early impressionable puppy stage, have implacable characters, and it seems to me that one of the best things about our relationship with dogs is how we have to figure out ingenious ways to work around their rather rigid likes and dislikes. It stretches us in ways we would otherwise not be stretched. Mrs. Thurber probably never dreamed she would invent a machine to replicate the sound of thunder, and that she would be standing at her back door of an evening and using it to get her beloved, though monstrous, dog back into the house.

James Thurber's dog Muggs

December 21

I decided to pre-empt the early-morning biting by taking the dog to the big box hardware store to buy a baby gate to block off the stairs. Her new favourite game is racing up the stairs at full tilt, especially now that my mother has arrived for the holidays. Fig is very curious to see what my mother is up to in the spare room.

It's just before Christmas, but early in the morning, the box store was mostly empty. A burly employee with dog bones tattooed on his forearms came to see the puppy. He was so shy that when he talked to us, he kept his eyes on the floor. When I was at the cash, I put Fig up on the counter while I paid, and she stood stock still. Perhaps the height of the counter reminded her of the vet. The cashier made a fuss of her and the puppy tried to eat the credit card receipt as it spooled out of the machine. New things tire Fig out, so she napped in the car on the way home.

A mild day today, so I picked up some of the masses of dog shit in my tiny yard, and I'm taking her over to play with my partner's dog this afternoon because it's warm enough for them to run around outside. It is nice to have a momentary break from winter. Nancy's dog is a two-year-old rescue from the Dominican Republic named Ranger. She was a street dog and her scrappy temperament is a perfect match for the rambunctious Fig.

A puppy feels like a kind of disaster and all response to it is in the disaster mode. All reaction. Mostly I try to avoid being bitten by the puppy and to find ways to tire her out. The tiring out part is not much different from how one deals with a toddler, but the biting part is an added challenge.

But there is a change today. Some of my lessons are sticking, and I realize it's all because the dog likes me more. It was hard for her to care about not biting me hard when I meant nothing to her, but she is starting to come to me for comfort and affection, not to mention food, so I matter more to her and she is invested more in not hurting me.

A vizsla's eyes are blue at birth and turn gold as the dog gets older. There is no white in the eye—the eye is the same colour as the fur, so they can be invisible to their prey when hunting. All the parts of the vizsla match—eye colour, fur, and toenails, all of it a rich reddish-gold hue. I notice today that Fig's eyes are beginning to darken and are not the pale blue they were a week ago.

We were up at five today. Since the puppy has been here, I've watched the sunrise each morning. Also, I'm listening to more music because it calms the dog to have the radio on. I am glad that Fig likes music because it is something that has increasingly become important to me, having come from a musical family. Listening to music is a way to remember my brother and my father.

While I wait to have Fig's character revealed to me, I realize that perhaps she is waiting for the same thing. We are possibly both waiting for traits to emerge in the other that feel familiar or sympathetic to us. Commonality goes a long way to producing empathy. In writing my novels, I try and find something in common with my characters, whether they are real or imagined, and this makes it easier to relate to them, to inhabit them. This is usually the way in for me, as it's very difficult to imagine being someone you have absolutely nothing in common with. I learned this early on in writing—that shape-shifting is possible, but only if there is something recognizable in the shape you're shifting into. I know, from talking with other writers, that this is a tactic many of us employ when we are writing character.

Maybe Fig recognizes that music is what we have in common.

STRUCTURE

I found my first vizsla in my thirties. Before that, I hadn't been able to afford a dog, barely surviving myself on what I made from my three part-time jobs after I moved out of my parents' house. They continued to have dogs, however, first one golden retriever and then another. I remember my father becoming so upset when the first one died that he had to go out the next day and get another dog to immediately replace her.

My first vizsla was my first dog as an adult. After much debating, my partner at the time and I decided on this breed because they had many traits that we considered highly desirable. Vizslas are not big droolers—the memory of Lisa's constant drooling has remained fresh in my mind for decades now—nor are they excessive bark-ers, like Timmy had proven himself to be. They don't require much, if any, grooming, aside from nail clipping, and they are the only dogs without an odour. They are athletic and extremely bonded to their humans. Vizs-las are intelligent and adapt well to new situations and places. Also, they are exceedingly good-looking and have been called the super models of the dog world. Not that this should matter, but as Keats so aptly put it, "[a] thing of beauty is a joy forever."

At the time we were researching breeds, vizslas were not a very popular dog in Canada. We had never seen one in the flesh, and the first one we met was Dash, the mother of Hazel.

To welcome the new puppy to our home, I spent ages sewing her a rug out of some leftover sheepskin I had from my motorcycle seat. I thought it was important that I make something for the new dog, and I had a fantasy of how the puppy would look curled up asleep on the cozy rug.

When we went to pick up the puppy, she didn't want to be separated from her mother and screamed when we took her into the car, scratching frantically on the window glass in a heartbreaking attempt at escape. Back at the house, she ripped apart my gift of the sheepskin rug in a frenzied fury.

All the books we had read talked about how the new puppy would bond immediately with us, but it was clear, for weeks, that the puppy hated us and just wanted to be back with her mother and littermates. She regularly drew blood from me, and from anyone who dared visit, leaping straight up at the gate we used to barricade her in the kitchen, and snapping her razor-sharp teeth down over any unprotected flesh.

Hazel was born in the late fall, so she was a winter puppy. We lived in Ottawa then and the year of the new puppy was also the coldest winter on record, so it was fairly impossible to take her outside in the beginning, and equally impossible to exhaust her indoors. But when spring came, I was able to walk her in the Arboretum, a beautiful spot by the Rideau Canal with woods and hills and, as the name suggests, lots of different varieties of trees.

At the Arboretum, if I was there early enough in the morning, there was sometimes a woman who walked four Irish wolfhounds. They would appear out of the early morning mist, like an image from a Russian novel— four shaggy ghosts, moving slowly across the dewy grass.

The woman walked them early in the morning because the dogs were naturally shy and didn't like to meet any other dogs or humans.

At the Arboretum, there was also a very aristocratic-looking woman who owned a greyhound. Sometimes I would see her near the pond. She would unclip the leash from her greyhound and say, in a very posh British voice, "Race for Mistress, Adam," and the greyhound would dutifully tear up and down the field in front of her.

At the pond, I would often see uncommon (to me) birds, such as a green heron or a black-crowned night heron. There was a small chalkboard attached to a wall of the shed near the edge of the parking lot and people would write down birds they had seen, so I could use the list to look for specific birds, as well as verify what I had spotted myself.

Hazel loved the Arboretum, and she would mostly trot companionably along with me through the fields and woods. But once, in winter, she raced up the snowy hill to attack the toboggans (a thing she had never seen before) that were, unfortunately, filled with small children. And once, in summer, she raced up that same hill to launch herself into the middle of a picnic that a mother was having with her young children. Before we could get to her, she ate all their food and bounced around on their picnic blanket while they screamed in terror.

The nature of Hazel, in the beginning anyway, was not an easy nature. She insisted on flying out the back door, barking, to clear the yard of any cats or squirrels, and did this all her life, whatever yard she was in, whether it was day or night. To cut her nails, I had to lie right on top of her, fight her in fact, before she would allow me to use the clippers on her feet. She did not like her feet touched, or her ears. She was a constant roller in dead things— squirrels or fish mostly, although once, most horrifyingly, a large puddle of human vomit. Spring would uncover what had been dead all winter in the woods, and Hazel couldn't wait to find any rotting animal corpse and roll in it. (My vet calls these newly thawed corpses "spring pâté.") She hated any noise that sounded like a gunshot. In the beginning, this was pretty much confined to actual gunshots and fireworks, but as she aged, the category expanded to include tree branches cracking, car doors slamming, a book snapping shut. It turns out there are many, many sounds that resemble a gunshot and Hazel was afraid of all of them. If she heard one while she was on a walk, she would hightail it back to the car, without a backwards glance to see if we were following. Luckily, she became deaf later in life and wasn't bothered anymore by the sounds that had terrified her so much when she was a younger dog.

Gunshots aside, Hazel grew into a terrific companion. She was great in a canoe or on the hiking trail, and game for anything. When she was over eleven, she did a late-summer canoe trip with me where we had a dozen portages in a single day, and the dog hopped obligingly in and out of the canoe and walked them all. She always kept pace with me on the trails as I schlepped various packs and barrels between one lake and the next. If I slowed down when I was portaging, she slowed down as well, so that we were always walking exactly together.

In the car, she sat beside me in the passenger seat, looking dismissively out at all the pedestrians. She had a very snooty expression, common to the breed, but also very particular to her. Once, I was photographed for a magazine article on a novel I had written about the relationship between Julia Margaret Cameron, the Victorian photographer, and her housemaid Mary Hillier. The magazine photographer came to my house and, because he liked the look of Hazel, included her in the photograph. When the article came out, it had the headline "A Lady and Her Maid" and it showed me sitting on my living room couch, with the dog looming behind me, looking very aristocratic and snobby, making it seem obvious to the viewer as to who was the "Lady" and who was the "Maid."

VIZSLAS COME BY their snobbery naturally. Traditionally, they were the hunting and companion dogs of the Hungarian aristocrats, and the only dogs they allowed indoors. The stories have it that when the Hungarian aristocrats were fleeing the Turkish armies, they went by horse and sled over the Carpathian Mountains, their vizslas wrapped in furs on their laps. The breed almost died out in World War II during the Russian occupation, as the dogs were killed by both the Nazis and Russian soldiers because they were a symbol of the Hungarian aristocracy. After the war ended, there were only about a dozen dogs left in Hungary, and the breed was brought back from dying out by U.S. breeders.

The vizsla is a high-energy dog that needs a lot of

off-leash exercise and becomes bored easily. They form intense, close bonds with their people and often follow you everywhere, even to the bathroom. They are not easy dogs, but I like that about them. I'm bored by dogs that just lie around like living rugs, and those who are too obliging and seem to have no will of their own, or who will chase a ball or stick endlessly. Hazel would chase a stick exactly once and then tire of the enterprise.

Aside from having a lot of will, Hazel had a healthy sense of self-preservation. Once, when we were walking together over ice, close to shore, I fell in. It wasn't that deep where I was, only up to my thighs, so I was able to scramble out easily enough. But Hazel, at the sight of me crashing through the ice, ran straight for land, with no concern at all for my well-being. Unlike any of those *Dogs You'd Like to Meet,* she did not run for help, or wade in to try and rescue me, dragging a life preserver or length of rope to where I was flailing around on the ice.

After I managed to crawl out of the icy water and walk stiffly back to the car, all the hinges of my body slowly freezing shut, I found the dog sitting patiently by the driver's door, waiting to be let into the warm interior.

Hazel might have loved herself first, but she did love

her human companions second. I came to depend on her, and there were many occasions when she saved the day. Once, a friend and I were on a hike at the end of October. We had underestimated how long the hike would take and hadn't left enough time for it, considering that the daylight was reduced at this point in the autumn. We found ourselves in the woods at nightfall, a good five kilometres or so from the trailhead. We had, stupidly, not brought a flashlight, and once the sun went down, we couldn't see the trail anymore. We had reconciled ourselves to sleeping out in the woods—it wasn't a cold night and we had enough water and some food—and beginning the walk again in the morning, but Hazel had no wish to sleep all night outdoors and so she kept moving along the trail. She was old at this point, eleven or twelve, and her face had turned entirely white. She would move along the trail, then turn to see if we were coming, and each time she turned, her face flashed white like a light, and we were able to follow her all the way out in this way, with her turning towards us and waiting for us to catch up, and then moving slowly on again, her white face as bright as the moon through the trees.

She was always a strong dog, with lots of stamina.

Even on the day she died, at the age of thirteen, she went for an hour-long walk first.

Hazel and I moved houses a lot in the time we were together. One of the places we lived in was a small white house that was opposite a large city park. In the summer, we would get up early and I would walk out in my bare feet with the dog. No need for a leash or collar, or shoes for myself. We were always the only creatures up and in the park that early, and I remember the languid feeling of our slow walk over the morning grass, the companionable ease we had together by then.

Happiness is a hard thing to describe, because even though the circumstances of various joys are different, the feeling is much the same and there is something oddly banal in attempts to translate it into something that can be explained to others. But happiness, true happiness, is also fairly rare in a life, and I have clear memories of the moments when it has existed in mine. Walking over the summer grass with Hazel was one of these moments, as was heading out the front door with my subsequent dog, Charlotte, for our morning walk. It is such a simple thing, walking with or after the dog, watching them take in all the smells and sights of the day. I'm not sure why it conjures up such happiness in me. But like all the happy times I can remember in my life, it is about a sense of being notched fully into the present moment, with no thought or desire outside of that. It is about belonging completely to the briefness of my own life—which is disappearing by degrees with every step I take—and wanting nothing else.

December 22

Still a week to go before the puppy gets her second set of shots and I can take her for some limited walks outside. It will be hard to keep her contained until then. Her confidence is growing and she wants to explore more of her world. I spent ages this morning trying to block off the area under the deck out back, and then she spent ages trying to wriggle through the barricade. We are at odds in terms of where she is allowed to go and where she wants to go.

Worst biting incident so far today: Her little needle teeth hooked into one of my nostrils and ripped a section of skin and cartilage. Lots and lots of blood. She also bit my mother, who is on blood thinners for her heart, and things have looked a bit like a murder scene in the house today. My mother, from years of dealing with her own dogs, is very sanguine about Fig and concentrates more on what she sees as the sweet nature of the dog, rather than on her biting attacks.

Everything could be solved by exhausting Fig outside, but because she doesn't have her second set of vaccines, I can do nothing but let her rampage around for a while inside, and then throw her into her crate for a spell to cool down. The puppy energy is so frenetic, but I can see that she is in the grips of it, as am I, and that she doesn't really have much control over herself yet. The biting frenzy of the baby vizsla is so common to the breed that owners have given the attacks a term: *sharkies*.

Just a year ago, Charlotte was still alive. She would have greeted my mother's visit with some excited snuffling and tail wagging, and then she would have gone back to lying on the couch, or sleeping in front of the fire. The house was firmly hers as well as mine, and she operated in it with great independence—going in and out whenever she wanted through the half-open back door, taking herself upstairs to bed in the evening when she was tired. She was more of a roommate than a creature I had to watch and mind, and she made good decisions, so

I never had to worry about what she was doing. She was sensible right from puppyhood.

What a difference a year makes! Now I do practically nothing but watch Fig and try to keep her out of trouble. She seems the opposite of sensible, and I wonder if I am doing enough to keep her in line. Perhaps she needs more structure?

I STARTED WRITING A NOVEL just before I had my first dog. After my earlier attempt in England, I hadn't planned on ever writing a novel again, as ever being anything other than a poet. But I had an idea about a pair of women pilots in the 1930s that didn't fit into the poem or short story category, so I wrote the novel to fit the idea.

Leaving Earth was my first published novel. It sold into a lot of countries, was optioned for film, and made it possible for me to spend at least half of my time writing instead of pumping gas or painting houses.

The research for that book was very physical. I went up in a small plane to fly the route of my fictional pilots. I made a facsimile cockpit, using a chair and the dimensions of the real cockpit of a Moth biplane, so that I could practise moving around in the small space my pilots occupied. I became a kind of method writer, trying to experience as much of the story as was possible.

Because *Leaving Earth* is based on the exploits of real pilots, and because many of my subsequent books are similarly based on either real people or real events, I had to decide from the beginning of my novels what I was going to be faithful to in terms of the research. I learned quite quickly that it is impossible to get everything right, and determining what to be faithful to becomes a choice, like all the other choices that go into writing a novel. In *Leaving Earth*, I decided to be faithful to the physical realities of my fictional pilots, hence the preoccupation with the size of the Moth cockpit and the flight in the small plane over the route I intended the women to fly in my novel. I was also faithful to the abilities and limitations of the plane and to all of the mechanical aspects of the flight, including the weather for the period of my novel, which I had researched through the Environment Canada archives.

What I wasn't faithful to was the characters of the pilots. Even though the flight was based on a real flight, I moved it to Canada from the United States, and I invented the pilots completely. Also, endurance flights with two pilots tended to be undertaken in planes with an enclosed cockpit, but I wanted the open cockpit in my book because part of the story was about the communication between the women, and it is much harder to communicate in an open cockpit with the wind tearing the words out of your mouth as soon as you utter them.

When doing the research for the book, I befriended a contemporary of Amelia Earhart, a woman from California named Bobbi Trout. (She had nephews named Brook and Lake.) Bobbi had done one of the early endurance flights and had been at the beginning of women's aviation in America. Her pilot's licence was signed by Orville Wright. She was in her late eighties when I knew her and still had perfect eyesight. She drove a red Porsche fast along the California coast highways, and she told me that Amelia Earhart hadn't been a very good pilot, spending too much time promoting herself rather than putting in the flying hours. "It was no surprise to me that she got lost," she said.

I would talk to Bobbi late at night. She was forgetful of the time difference and often called me after I'd gone to bed. I liked lying there, still half-asleep, listening to Bobbi's raspy voice recounting flying stories. I used many of her experiences for my fictional pilots with her blessing. She used to despair to me over the phone that she'd had all these amazing adventures but whenever she tried to put them into words, they sounded banal.

Having been a poet, and having published three books of poetry before my first novel, made me a very image-based novelist, from all the years of writing in an image-centred way. It also meant that I tended towards brevity—a tendency that I have maintained. *Leaving Earth* is full of short scenes because I couldn't figure out how to write long. I couldn't figure out how to transition from one scene to the next, so I simply ended a scene and moved on to another one. This made the pace fairly quick, which, luckily for me, suited the story I was telling, so the short scenes don't betray my lack of ability, and instead seem to be there as a deliberate device.

Leaving Earth is the only one of my novels written without my having a dog. I wrote it in the city in which the book is set, Toronto, and the story is very city-oriented. What happened when I started living with Hazel is that the countryside, which because of the dog became a necessary component of my life, started to creep into my work.

By the time I was writing my next novel, *Afterimage*, I had separated from my partner and was living in an apartment above an office building that was being renovated. Every day, underneath my feet, ducts were being hammered in or walls knocked down. It was noisy and messy and the middle of summer. My apartment was unbearably hot and there was no outside space. I had one fan and turned it on the dog, who lay dolefully on my bed, her face pressed right up to the blades that swirled the tepid air.

I had no phone installed, and cellphones weren't in existence in a common way, so if anyone wanted to get ahold of me, they had to stand in the alley behind the building and yell up for me.

All day, I sweated over my novel, the floor shaking beneath my feet as the renovations went on below. At night, after dark, when it was finally cooler out, I took Hazel through the streets for a walk in the nearby park. We would set out around ten and return about midnight.

Because I had Hazel full-time on my own now, and because there was no adjoining outside space where I was living, my days had to have structure, and that structure had to revolve around the dog's needs.

I was realizing, with the new-found shape to my daily life, that I also needed to work at structure in my novel. Structure was what would enable me to be able to write myself out of one scene and into the next. It is a scaffold that ensures the building won't collapse and keeps all the parts in their respective places, allowing easy movement between them.

The part of *Afterimage* I was working on in the apartment was a section set in winter. All day I suffered from the heat and the noise while simultaneously existing in Victorian England in the middle of winter. The disconnect between my actual life and the life of the novel was a big one, but I was able to keep the two worlds separate and didn't feel any discomfort in doing so. This gets harder to do with age. Things meld together more, or long to be together more. It becomes harder and less appealing to compartmentalize oneself. Perhaps because time has shortened—there is less ahead than there used to be—the desire to live wholly in the moment one is actually inhabiting is great, because there will be fewer moments to come.

On one of the late-night walks with the dog at the end of summer, we strolled past a little white house for sale, and I went to look at it the following day. The moment I stepped inside, I loved it, and I was so confident of this feeling that I didn't even go and look at the upstairs before I made an offer. The realtor assured me that I would get the house as there had been no other offers and I was willing to pay the asking price.

But at the last minute, another offer did come in, and I lost the house. Hazel and I would walk by every evening that fall and look through the front window at the new owner sitting watching TV in the living room. He had oversized furniture, completely wrong for the small house, and I couldn't understand why he was there instead of me. But finally, I resigned myself to losing the house and began unpacking all my books at the apartment, something I had put off when I initially landed there, leaving them in a wall of boxes between the kitchen and living room. When the last book was on the shelves, and I had reconciled myself to being where I was, the doorbell rang and it was the realtor from the little white house. She asked if I still wanted it. She told me that the new owner had bought it to live there temporarily while he waited for another house to be built for him, and as this had now happened, he was offering the white house to me.

I planted my first garden at this house, and I wrote two of my favourite books there, *The Lost Garden* and *Wild Dogs*.

Leaving Earth had been shaped from research, much of it experiential. *Afterimage* was firmly a product of my imagination. But *The Lost Garden* and *Wild Dogs* were books that were influenced by the physicality of living with Hazel.

The Lost Garden was the most enriching writing experience that I have ever had. I was ecstatically happy while writing the book because the writing was effortless. I actually wrote the final two pages of the book first and then worked towards them from the beginning, barely changing a word of those final pages when I reached them again. The whole thing felt like a kind of miracle. I finished the first draft in ten weeks and barely had to alter a word of it for publication.

Virginia Woolf described writing as stumbling after one's own voice. Certainly, the experience of writing *The Lost Garden* felt like that to me. I moved so quickly towards what I wanted to say that I was barely conscious of saying it. I had found my voice, which, for me, wasn't just a question of finding the right words to tell a story, but was also about discovering the emotions behind the words, and letting those emotions propel the language.

It is easy to distrust what comes easily, to think that more effort is required to make something worthwhile. But, in my experience of writing, the easier it comes, the better it is. The work that is laboured over for years, picked apart and put back together again, is the work that is probably not that good and never was. There is no shame in giving up what isn't working. It is often a better solution than hammering away at something that is never going to be very good.

Also, I believe that the experience of the writer and the reader are similar, in that the speed at which a book is written is often the speed at which it is read. So, if you spend ten years writing your book, it could very well take someone ten years to read it.

In *The Lost Garden*, I wrote about an encyclopedia of roses called *The Genus Rosa*, written by Ellen Willmott. My main character, Gwen, lies under this book, using it to approximate the weight of a human body. It's a rare book now, but I managed to obtain one through inter-library loan, and I would lie under this enormous folio myself every morning before I began writing, waiting for the words to bubble up in me, until the moment where I would leap up and go to my desk to write them down.

I lay under *The Genus Rosa*, walked the dog, planted a garden, and wrote my novel at breakneck speed. In the early mornings, I would walk out barefoot with Hazel. We could cross the road in front of my little white house and walk through a series of interconnected parks down to the lake and back, all before anyone else was up. Walking the dog became the punctuation in the writing day, and often on those walks, I worked out some concern in the book, or a phrase would suddenly occur to me that I would write down when I returned to the house.

Dogs live very firmly in their bodies. Writing is very much about the life of the mind. So, having to cross over from one state to another, while jarring at first, actually opened up the writing process for me. If I just sat at my desk until my pen ran dry, it would have been harder to keep going. But by taking frequent breaks to go outside and exercise my body while walking the dog, I came back to my task of the book refreshed. I would start writing *The Lost Garden* after the first walk of the day, and I would keep going, punctuated by dog walks every few hours, right up until I went to bed at night. The walk breaks refreshed me and I never felt tired from the amount of writing that I was doing.

Structure in a novel, and in life, is the perfect balance of order and chaos. The structure of a day could be the four dog walks undertaken at regular intervals throughout that day. But no walk will be the same as the next. Each one, even if it happens along the exact same route as the previous walk, will yield up a different combination of sightings and experiences. Similarly, a novel could be structured around fifty-two sections, each one representing a specific week of a year. This is a fairly strict structure, and yet what happens within those individual sections could be wildly diverse. I believe that the creative freedom inherent in this mix of the expected and the unexpected makes for the best writing.

When I was thinking up my next novel, *Wild Dogs*, I decided to structure it after the way that a dog turns and turns before settling down to sleep. I wanted the story to turn like that, to circle back on itself and then continue again before coming to rest. The novel is about dogs, or rather it is about our relationship with dogs, about wildness and domesticity and belonging. With this novel, I was moving deeper into my own relationship with dogs, having them infuse my writing sentence by sentence.

In a way, *Wild Dogs* depended on my knowing what it would feel like to be a dog. And so I used to run through the forest with Hazel, vaulting fallen logs and cresting hills, my lungs burning and heart pounding—Hazel leading me enthusiastically deeper into the wilderness. One memorable day, we came upon a hawk carrying a squirrel. The squirrel was almost too heavy for the bird, and the hawk couldn't get the height it needed, so it flew just in front of us through the trees at head level. Without thinking, both the dog and I gave chase simultaneously— the dog wanting to catch the hawk, and me to keep the wondrous sight in view for as long as possible.

Living with Hazel taught me the benefit of balancing the physical world of the dog with the interior writing life, and the wildness of the dog reinforced my own sense of wildness, and gave me a sense of freedom as well as companionship. I think too that it kept my ideas fresh, because I couldn't complacently sink into writerly habits. My being was constantly being shaken out of its routine by the needs of the dog to be a dog, to run through the woods, or notice the movement of other animals. Having a dog and living some of the time on the dog's terms kept me immersed in the physical world. A part of me could always be animal in the company of the dog, and this kept me engaged with nature, with the life force, which is also the creative force.

Hazel and me

GERTRUDE STEIN and Alice B. Toklas had three white standard poodles in succession, each one called Basket, after the first one, so named because Stein thought he would look good carrying a basketful of flowers—which is something he never actually did.

The dogs operated as muses to Stein, who said of the second Basket that she worked out the difference between sentences and paragraphs from listening to him drinking from his water bowl. The difference, noted by Alice B. Toklas in her autobiography, was that ". . . paragraphs are emotional and sentences are not."

The Baskets were well-documented and were photographed with Stein by Cecil Beaton and Man Ray, enjoying, or not enjoying, their own measure of fame alongside the famous experimental writer.

Gertrude Stein holding a portrait of Basket while the real Basket looks on

December 23

Fig likes to eat dirt. She likes to eat the splinters of wood on the edges of the fireplace logs. She likes to bark in a shrill voice at the fireplace poker where it lies on the hearth. She likes to rip paper into tiny shreds. She likes to tear the nose off her stuffed animals and ferociously pull out the stuffing. She likes to run upstairs but has no idea how to get back down the long flight from the second floor to the main floor. She likes to go into holes and under furniture. When I opened my spice cupboard today, she dove inside, thinking it was a portal to somewhere more interesting. She likes shoes, and especially their laces. She likes watching the lights of the cars disappear down the street, and the blue jays that land on the porch roof and then fly off again. She likes visitors.

Fig does not like being told to stop biting. She does not like to be kept inside when she could be exploring outside. She does not like loud sneezes, or when I am talking on the phone. She does not like the baby gate I use to block off the bottom of the staircase. She does not like big dogs. She does not like to wait. She does not like to be told what to do.

STRUCTURE, FOR A WRITER living with a dog, also becomes about how the writer goes about training their dog. For Maurice Sendak, children's author and illustrator, the German shepherd was his dog of choice. He got his dogs from the Monks of New Skete, who are based in Cambridge, New York, and are famous for their dog-training methods. The monks published two

Maurice Sendak and Herman (© Mariana Cook 2005)

popular books on the subject. They advocate, among other things, that a dog is not an inferior being, but rather an equal one, and should be treated with respect. Puppies at New Skete are never alone; each one is tied to a rope that is fastened around the waist of a monk, who goes about his daily business with the puppy trailing along behind him.

Sendak let the monks train the dogs and got them when they were adults. He didn't like to know the age of his dogs, because this would make him worry about their dying. His last, and perhaps favourite, German shepherd was named Herman, after Herman Melville.

When we first got Hazel, we read the New Skete training books. I have forgotten much of what the monks wrote about dog training, but it might be time to get them out again and see what I might try with Fig.

January 3

The puppy had an upset stomach and all house-training progress has been lost. The dining room rug, after absorbing multiple accidents, has now been rolled up and sent to the cleaners. Felt very much like a backwards day with no forward progress at all. I am feeling very discouraged by everything. Also, now that Fig has been peeing and shitting in the house, she is reluctant to go to the cold outdoors and tries to run away when I want her to go outside into temperatures in the minus twenties.

My mother left after the holidays, and Fig whined for her when she stepped into her car and drove away. The puppy is attaching to her life and the people in it, but the biting is still hard for us to bear. Also, she has discovered that she can find shoes in the hallway, and she likes to drag those into the living room to chew on. A lot of time spent wrestling them away from her and trying to block off the hallway. Tiresome. At what point does one age out of dealing with babies?

I left her in her crate in the house by herself for an hour while I went out to lunch. I worried that she would cry or wake up and be afraid not to hear movement around the house. But when I came home, she was sound asleep. Driving back along the street towards the house, I realized I had missed her while I was out. So, we are attaching to each other, I guess, in a Stockholm Syndrome kind of way. It seems to be happening simultaneously. There is no difference between her feeling for me and my feeling for her. We are moving at the same rate towards one another.

STRUCTURE IS ABOUT setting rules for a story and then following them. But first, one has to decide what those rules will be. Does it make sense to impose a rigid structure on a novel that is more experimental in nature? No, better to have a looser hold on the narrative there, let it drift around more naturally. Structure is a kind of discipline and not everything needs the same kind of treatment.

Emily Brontë's dog, Keeper, was her companion on her walks across the bleak Yorkshire moors. Half mastiff and half bulldog, Keeper's size alone was a deterrent to anyone who might wish Emily trouble.

The huge dog came to the parsonage as an adult, given to them by a man who warned that Keeper didn't like to be told what to do or disciplined, and that he would attack anyone who tried. Because of this warning, the Brontës didn't try to curb Keeper, and he did as he pleased, napping on their beds and growling if anyone tried to get him to move off.

Painting of Keeper by Emily Brontë

One day, Emily objected to his muddying her bedspread and lost her temper with him, beating him savagely with her fists around his face. The dog, surprised at the sudden attack, didn't defend himself. Afterwards, Emily tended his injuries, and from that moment forward, they were devoted to each other. When Emily died at the age of thirty, Keeper followed the coffin to the churchyard and slept for the rest of his life outside Emily's old room, sometimes lifting his head to howl in sorrow.

It is, of course, never a good idea to physically discipline a dog. But there is something about that story, about the relationship between Emily Brontë and Keeper that strikes me. It seems to me that the natures of the dog and the human were similarly stubborn and violent, and the clash that happened between them was really the only thing that could have brought them both to this understanding and given them the mutual respect that was needed to cement their bond.

January 4

The stomach upset became more serious and I took Fig to the vet. She is now on antibiotics and they are testing her stool to make sure that she doesn't have something life-threatening like parvo. Now that I have bonded more with the dog, the thought that she is ill is very distressing. The vet switched her food to a gastro wet food from the puppy kibble that she was mostly eating, although sometimes ignoring. She is not a very food-focused dog yet, and will only eat all of her food if I play a game like I am interested in eating it myself. Charlotte would do anything for food, anything at all, so it feels odd to have a dog who isn't totally interested in eating.

Carried her through the park again this morning, before the worst of her illness. Saw a barred owl and four deer in the top field. Fig followed a squirrel with her eyes, and some chickadees, but didn't seem very interested in the deer and didn't notice the owl.

Tonight she was more low-key and has slept a lot. I cradled her on my lap while I read some of the monks' book on dog training. What I remember from the book about the monks' appreciation for dogs as fully sentient beings is there, but some of the corrective training methods read as harsh to me now. The monks advocate shaking dogs by the scruff of their necks and cuffing them under their chins, and also rolling alphas onto their backs to show the dogs who's boss. There is no treat training or training by positive reinforcement, no building of mutual trust. The relationship between the monks and their dogs is hierarchical and depends on the dogs' subservience. Structure, in terms of the dog training advocated by the monks, means discipline. I think of structure more in terms of building an armature of routine that will guide and support a dog and allow trust to develop. In writing, structure holds the story in place. In living with dogs, structure holds the relationship between human and dog together.

I stop reading and close the book, stroke Fig's silky ears and watch her small ribcage rise and fall with her breathing.

SOME WRITERS CREATE an imagined structure for their dogs, based on their personalities. Zora Neale Hurston had two dogs, with the very simple names of Shag and Spot. In a letter to a friend, she described their characteristics in terms of the jobs that would suit them.

SHAG: the female puppy would make an excellent maid and child-nurse. Vacuum cleaner tongue that would keep all dust under the carpet and wash the

Zora Neale Hurston with friends and one of her dogs

baby ten times a day. Allow no weeds in yard nor garden, in fact, allow nothing whatever to grow. Great digger, and could be very serviceable to construction company as a bull-dozer or tractor, etc.

SPOT: Make an excellent straw-boss or foreman. Takes no orders from anyone, but prepared to give out plenty. General Motors, Ford, and Standard Oil take notice, etc. Mind already made up on every subject in the world. Orders all ready to give out. Even orders guests to go home when she gets tired, and enforces her orders by going around and nipping each one on the heel. New hostess approach to guest-disposal. Prepared to teach it at a reasonable rate.[12]

January 5

Fig is soon back to normal. Can't tell if it's the drugs and the new food or if things just resolved on their own. Relieved, but then annoyed at her crazy energy levels and the constant biting. Sometimes, when she is particularly crazy, she just stands there and snaps her jaws at me. There is very little control over anything at this age—temper, bowels, emotions of any kind.

We listened to a lot of music today, in our isolation. Fig seems partial to piano music and is agitated by guitar.

There is meant to be an ice storm tonight. All I am thinking about is that it can't delay her second set of shots in two days, because I can't bear this crazy level of pent-up energy much longer. The moment we can go outside will be a very sweet one and can't come soon enough. I hope the storm isn't as bad as they are predicting, and that I am able to take Fig to the vet when it is over.

January 6

The dog was terrible yesterday, but today she is good and has spent much of the day sleeping. There is a lot of up and down with a puppy, none of which I seem to have remembered from previous puppies.

There was an ice storm in the night and it was slippery taking the puppy out for the middle-of-the-night pee. Fig, who has never seen ice before, spent some of the morning sampling the flakes of it clinging to the back steps.

When the dog is calm and not biting, I appreciate her more, but I was thinking today that although we are bonding, I still have no idea who she is. She seems so controlled by her puppy hormones and her still-developing brain. Personality is something so much more subtle than hormones.

The sound of the icy branches clinking against one another in the wind is pleasant, like bells, or the tips of masts touching in the harbour when the sea is on the boil.

The momentous day arrived, and after Fig had her second set of shots, I took her for a little walk in the woods, where I was pretty certain that we would not meet other dogs, because until she has her third and final set of shots, she's not completely safe from unvaccinated dogs. Unfortunately, the ice storm was giving its last gasp and it was sleeting out and very cold and unpleasant. Even though the walk was only about fifteen minutes in length, Fig couldn't understand why we were doing it and shivered and shook the whole way, eventually pawing at me to pick her up and carry her. So, it wasn't the fantasy walk I had imagined, but at least we have started down that road, as it were. The daily walks will give the much-needed structure to the puppy's life, and that will do much to expand both of our worlds.

PROCESS

Perhaps walking with a dog, being in the company of a dog, is also about our desire to become more animal ourselves? I wrote about this in *Wild Dogs*, and I think about it a lot. That novel came about because I found a newspaper article that detailed an attack on a jogger by a pack of wild dogs, and in the article, it was noted that a pet dog can become wild in as little as two weeks. Could that happen to Hazel, my dog at the time? Would she forget our close bond in as little as two weeks, given the opportunity to run unfettered through the forest in the company of her fellows? And conversely, what is it within human beings that is still wild, that still longs to be wild?

I've only met one person who tried to become an actual dog. Once, I was at a funeral of an older man who had died suddenly. He had a large family with multiple wives, ex-wives, and several sets of children. A certain amount of time had been allotted to each member of the family to speak at the memorial service, but all the available minutes were used up by the eldest daughter of the first wife. She told a long, rambling story about how her father's death had made her unbearably lonely, and that all she wanted to do was to be a dog. (She had several Labrador retrievers with whom she lived.) So, she found some dog-like furry material and a seamstress who would sew her a dog suit, and every day she zipped herself into it and went outside with her dogs, splashing in the lake or nosing around the yard. She did whatever they did and, in this way, was able to bear her terrible grief over her father's death.

Because it was a funeral, no one dared laugh. And it wasn't so much that it was funny—although it was so outlandish that it *was* funny—but more that it was the strange turn this woman's grief had taken. There was something beautiful about her desire to be a dog and the effort she took to make it so. Although the one thought I had at the time was to wonder what her actual dogs made of it all, what they thought of her zipped into her dog suit, clumsily lurching after them around the yard.

While I have no desire to actually become a dog myself, I do admire many of their characteristics. Chief among these is their ability to be entirely inside a moment and then switch easily, and without regret, into another moment.

Perhaps one of the hardest things to learn about writing is that it is a continual process. Fixing words to a page doesn't mean that they are permanent and inflexible. You haven't arrived anywhere, even though it feels this way. For writing to have energy it has to remain energetic, and this means that it has to be able to move and change. After finally deciding on a train of thought, a line of words, it is an effort to shift direction.

But just as a dog has no trouble moving from one scent trail to another, twisting easily from the path she is on with no backwards glance, so a writer needs to be able to take off on another trail of ideas without worrying that they are heading in the wrong direction. To a dog, there is no wrong direction. There is just this moment and these interesting smells and sights, and then this next moment with more fascinating experiences. A dog is constantly in process, and I have learned much from their approach.

First, there is no wrong or right way to do things. There is just the way you are doing them—a way informed by craft but driven by instinct, feeling, and ideas. It's hard to keep judgment out of this mix, but to feel judgment or self-criticism means that you have stepped out of the moment you are in and are reflecting on it. So, like a dog on a trail, better to just keep your head down and keep going in the direction that has your interest and your feeling.

Good writing feels alive because it is alive—the writer hasn't been afraid to scrap a line or alter direction to find out what is happening in their story at the same time as they are writing it down on the page. It is exciting to write like this, to always be in motion. To be alive itself is to be "in process."

In terms of process, much can also be borrowed from a dog's life when writing about one.

Elizabeth Barrett Browning's cocker spaniel, Flush, was immortalized in poetry by Barrett Browning, and later in the novel *Flush* by Virginia Woolf. The much-cosseted spaniel had meals of cakes and macaroons and bits of beef, all hand-fed to him by Barrett. He apparently liked his bread slathered thickly with butter. Barrett was also teaching Flush the alphabet so that he could learn to read, and she was trying to teach him board games so that he might play them with her when she was confined to her sickroom.

When Robert Browning showed up to court Barrett and interrupted the close daily bond between mistress and dog, Flush bit Browning severely, twice. (He eventually reconciled himself to the union and became fond of Browning and accompanied him on walks.)

Flush was stolen and ransomed three times in his short life, and each time, Barrett Browning paid the full sum asked. The second time Flush was stolen, he was kept for six days in Whitechapel before being returned.

Barrett Browning wrote lovingly about and to her spaniel, and because she was often ill with various mysterious ailments, he was largely her only companion and thus assumed even greater importance in her affections.

Virginia Woolf, who also had cocker spaniels, made her biography of Flush part social commentary on Victorian society, giving Flush lots of opinions on everything that Virginia Woolf also had lots of opinions on. Woolf also drew on her own bond with her spaniel Pinka to talk imaginatively about cross-species communication be-

Virginia Woolf's novel
Flush, with her dog
Pinka on the cover

tween dogs and humans. The book was a bestseller when it was first published in 1933.

January 7

Another day, another short walk in the woods. This one was more pleasant because the weather was brighter and not spewing ice and snow from the sky the way it was yesterday. Some smelling was done and some tasting of moss. For a while, Fig carried around a dead leaf in her mouth. She seemed happier with the excursion, although introducing the outdoors is hard in the winter because of the cold. She will be surprised when summer comes and all the smells are released from the earth and the air is warm and languid. I try to imagine an older Fig, but the relentlessness of puppy Fig makes it almost impossible.

I transport her to the park in a small crate in the back seat of the car, and while she is always reluctant to get into the crate, she is often, when we reach the starting point of our woodsy walk, reluctant to get out. It is warm in the blanketed crate in the car and it is cold in the winter world, so there is some coaxing needed to make her exit her confines. I wonder when the walk will be the exciting thing and she will readily leave the warmth of the crate for the joys of the woods?

Fig had her first walk in the place where I used to walk Charlotte—her first walk where she wasn't carried for the majority of the time. It might have been a bit too far for her, as she was clearly tired by the end and I did carry her for a bit halfway through. But the day was mild and, overall, she did remarkably well. I let the leash drop a few times and we practised her recall, which she was very good at. It was a relief to be back out in the woods and not cooped up in the house, and I think she enjoyed the world of the forest. She carried a leaf for a while, then a stick, then a pine cone.

Home again and I gave her some egg with her food, which she wolfed down. I had thought I would let her sleep on me for a while, as is her wont, but she was acting crazy and biting a lot, so I put her in her crate and now she is sound asleep as I type this. The crazy biting sometimes means she is overtired, although it also means she is excited and wants to play. Puppyhood behaviour is very extreme.

We went to the first puppy class tonight, but it was a mixed bag. The other dogs were much older than Fig, some as much as five months old, and they were all large breeds, so she was unable to play much without getting hurt. One of the larger dogs actually jumped on her and sent her squealing for shelter underneath a chair. There was one large fluffy puppy that wasn't too bad, but it was disappointing overall. I wish they had arranged the classes according to the age of the puppies. Also, Fig's attention span isn't the greatest at the moment, so she was happiest just sitting watching the other puppies go through their paces, rather than doing "sit" or "stand" herself. Plus, she already knows how to sit and does it well and without my asking, so day one of puppy class felt a bit useless.

The instructor is a late-middle-aged woman with a tattoo of her dog's face on each of her calves and a very deep voice from years of cigarette smoking. She worked the room, coming and talking to each dog and owner. Fig and I were both mesmerized by her deep voice.

Sometimes the thing I hold out the most hope for is, in the end, disappointing. I had been waiting on puppy class to help with Fig's biting energy, but it wasn't the salvation I had been expecting. Fig was, understandably, reticent with the larger dogs and didn't really play with the rough-housing quality that I had been anticipating.

But the walk just before puppy class was a revelation of sorts, in that Fig discovered squirrels and the joy of chasing them. So, the world has opened up to contain her energy in a different way than the one I had imagined for her.

I ALWAYS LIKE THE QUESTIONS about process that people ask at a reading. It shows true engagement to ask about how something is made. And even that most basic of all process questions—Do you write by hand or on a computer?—has much to offer.

Writing by hand is slower—the pen doesn't go nearly as

quickly as the brain—but it is much more physical. There is the texture of the page, the slip of the ink over paper, the crossing out of lines or paragraphs and the way that looks to the eye. It is the thought process made visible.

Working on a computer is about chasing after ideas and phrases the moment they occur and racing hard to capture them exactly. The speed is intoxicating (if you are a fast typist) and the neatness of the script on the computer screen gives the words an authority that handwriting doesn't possess.

It also matters where you do your writing or typing, what sort of space you occupy, and whether there is a window where you are. I know writers who prefer to work in windowless rooms, in case the view distracts them. But I like the outside world bleeding in at the margins, and often when I have been unable to think of what to write, I have just described what is visible outdoors. Sometimes these little "distractions" have been the best part of whatever it is that I'm writing.

January 10

It's a freezing cold day today, too cold to really take the puppy out, so I bring her to one of the "Puppy Play" sessions at the dog school. Unfortunately, there was only one other dog there, a little terrier who had no interest in playing with Fig and attacked her whenever she attempted to play. It is discouraging that Fig can't find a dog who actually wants to play with her, rather than discipline her. I feel for her lonely little soul. She tried very hard to make the terrier play, and then sort of lost her temper and sat down on the floor, barking out of frustration. I admired her plucky attempts to make the impossible happen. She was the epitome of "dogged."

I took her back in the afternoon to another Puppy Play session, hoping for a different result. This time, there were two four-month-old puppies, but both large breeds—one a shepherd cross and one an Australian shepherd, so Fig was still overpowered. The whole situation is beginning to feel a bit like Goldilocks, in that the dogs are too big or too small or too aggressive or too uninterested. Fig spent much of the play session taking shelter under a chair.

A small bit of independence after dinner last night. Fig moved to one end of the couch and slept there, away from me. She has also taken to going to the front door in the evenings to look through the glass at the street beyond. She likes to watch the lights of the cars, and the odd person who walks by. She doesn't bark at them, but she is interested in watching them, or watching their movement past the house. I like this about her. Her focus is shifting slightly, away from me and more towards the larger world, illustrating how we all grow up, how it is about looking out and not being so caught up in the small swirl of the familiar, the inward, intimate world, but becoming curious about the mysterious outer world.

January 11

There was another ice storm in the night, and the shiny, slippery world is too treacherous to walk in this morning.

Fig continues to be interested in the outside world. She watched a man scrape off his entire car with an ice scraper this morning, intently watching every rise and fall of the scraper, and cocking her head to listen to the raspy sounds of the fragments of ice being dispatched from the windshield.

I was out of eggs, so I mixed a bit of oatmeal in with her kibble, and she seemed to like that as much as she has liked the eggs.

She sometimes wakes in the night and I can hear her amusing herself in her crate—chewing on something or rolling around. She never makes whining sounds to suggest that she wants to get out. I like that she is showing a lot of self-sufficiency. Charlotte was very independent and I am hoping that Fig will be as well.

Puppy class looms, but we haven't really practised anything from last week. Fig sits naturally for biscuits, so I don't bother to say the word, but probably, going forward, I should be more diligent. Dogs learn quickly, but humans always take a little longer. I fear I am treating the dog's school much the same way as I treated my own—never doing homework and then trying to just get by with minimal effort. Unfair to pass my terrible student habits on to the puppy. Who knows, maybe she wants to practise the lessons from last week? I think, not for the first time, that dogs are often hampered by their human companions.

SETTING

As Grizzle might have been the dog of Virginia Woolf's life, my next vizsla, Charlotte, was the dog of mine. She came into my life after a period of loss, so perhaps that helped to bond us. But mostly, I think, it was that our natures, while not so much similar, were entirely complementary. Charlotte was, as Virginia Woolf had noted about Grizzle, a dog of remarkable character, and I came to rely on her as much as, or more than, any of the humans in my life. She was calm and sensible, and she always could be depended upon to make calm and sensible decisions, whatever the situation.

For the first ten weeks Charlotte lived with me, I also had her sister Violet, who was to be the dog of a close friend. My friend had been out of the country for a year and wouldn't be able to collect the dog until she returned in early summer. It made sense for me to pick up both dogs from the breeder and keep them until my friend returned. It seemed like a good idea, that the puppies would be company for one another.

But as anyone who has had two puppies together knows, the dogs tend to bond with each other, instead of bonding strongly with the human. The puppies would look to each other when confronted with any new experience, or when deciding to cause mayhem. Everything was literally twice as hard with two puppies.

But we managed. We had our routines and we operated as a little pack. I crate-trained the puppies but put them together into the same crate, for company and because they were still so small. I slept downstairs with them for the first week, so that I could take them out to pee in the middle of the night. After that pee, I would let them come up on the couch with me for the remaining few hours of the night and we would snuggle together in a pile.

They were hard to manage in the city, so I took them most days up to the cabin that I used to part-own on a bit of river, and I tied the dogs to long bits of string. They tumbled over the grass, tried to drown one another in the river (by jumping on each other's heads), and were constantly getting tangled up. But they burned off a lot of energy, and we were all outside, so it was mostly good. Sometimes we slept together on the deck in the afternoons, with the May sun warming us through, and the fat bellies of the puppies rising and falling in a peaceful rhythm. (It was much easier having summer puppies than winter ones because of the amount of time we could be outdoors.)

We also spent a lot of time on the couch, both at the cabin and at home. It was a good way to separate the dogs so they weren't continually fighting and playing, to have one on one side of me and one on the other. I often had to have my hands touching them, to keep them under control, so reading was out of the question. I watched a lot of old episodes of *Law & Order*, sitting on the couch with the puppies. And Charlotte, who was always a devotee of routine, came to regard us sitting on the couch together as a norm that should be maintained at all costs. She never liked it if I worked upstairs in my office, and voiced her displeasure with a series of disciplinary grunts and pleading looks, until I gave in and conducted most of my working life from my end of the couch, while she lounged at her end, until she grew bored, or I grew bored, and then we would head outside for a walk.

It was hard to exercise the puppies, especially before they had all of their shots, but there was a thickly treed path down by the lake that was deserted in the early morning, and I would take them there. The path was narrow and the dense vegetation at the sides worked to funnel the puppies along in a line, so I could let them off their leashes and they would tumble along the path for a mile or so, at which point the path emptied into a field and they could frolic there for a while before being turned back for the return journey. I went very early in the morning so as not to meet any other people or dogs. The puppies were about ten weeks old at that point and looked like fat loaves of bread.

One morning, we were out there just after dawn. The light was slowly returning to the forest, like a thick syrup oozing between the trees. The puppies were more separated out than usual, with one running up ahead of me and one behind me. About halfway along the path, the puppy who was ahead of me (and I still don't know which dog it was, as they looked very similar as puppies) stopped and cocked her head to one side. I thought there must be someone behind us, so I turned as well and saw a huge coywolf about ten feet from the other puppy, creeping up and closing the distance fast.

I screamed for the puppies to come to me, which, miraculously, they did, and I was able to put leashes on them. The coywolf was put off by my screaming, but not stopped. He or she simply stepped into the vegetation at the side of the path but didn't leave.

I was flooded with the kind of fear that I imagine a prey animal feels most of the time, but the rush of adrenaline also made me suddenly aware of several things in that moment. I knew that the coywolf didn't want to hurt me, but he or she was hungry and did want to eat one of the puppies—that this course of action had been decided on and the coywolf was not going to be easily turned from the decision.

I started running along the path, back towards the car, dragging the puppies on their leads while the coywolf kept pace with us, about six feet away in the scrim of trees. Luckily, we weren't all that far from the car, so there wasn't a real opportunity for the coywolf to dart out and snatch one of the plump little puppies. We escaped and drove home.

To this day, I don't know which puppy alerted me to the presence of the coywolf, and which one would have been eaten. One dog saved the life of the other. Suddenly there was benefit to having the two dogs at once.

MY BROTHER DIED six months before I brought Charlotte home. He and Hazel actually died in the same week, and so the new dog was a very important part of healing for me. I wasn't able to write much at the time, but I was picking away at a memoir about my brother, just writing an extended letter to him, jotting things down when they occurred to me, but not thinking of it yet as a book.

Grief makes certain things impossible, and there's no telling what those things will be. I had low-level claustrophobia after Martin died. The indoors made me achy and restless, and I only felt better if I went outside. Walking was good, so I spent a lot of time walking with the new puppy and her sister. Their exuberant puppy happiness and excitement at all the new sights and sounds and smells of the world was energizing, and I was able to sort of stumble along in their wake. The natural world became even more important to me than it had before, and the smallest wonder in it was enough to calm my spirit for another day.

The summer after my brother died, the puppies, months old, boiled across the grass to the river. They were too energetic to be tied to their strings now, and so I had taken them to a friend's place, where there was more land to roam around on. The river was reached by crossing a field that contained cows, and there was always the danger of the cows and the dogs getting too interested in one another, but this particular morning, the cows were laced through the trees, and we had a clear run to the little strip of woods that bordered the river.

I had helped this friend cut trails on her property once, through thickets of prickly ash, through swamp, over slippery rock. But the trails, only recently made, were not used enough and were growing over quickly. The puppies were dwarfed by the weeds and tall grass, and romping through the vegetation exhausted them, so that by the time we got to the river, they didn't do their usual thing of trying to drown each other, but just splashed around at the edge of the water, making clumsy leaps after the frogs in the rushes.

As another friend of mine likes to say, "A tired dog is a

happy dog," and the return journey with the puppies was always much easier because they had spent themselves on the journey in. I had to carry them through the tall grass, and in the field, they lagged behind me, staggering along on their little puppy legs.

Because of this, because they were trailing behind me, I wasn't looking at them; I was looking out to the field, watching the horizon. Most of the cows still seemed to be grazing distantly among the maples, but there was one cow just to the left of us. At first, I had thought it was a rock, then I realized it was a cow lying on her side. When I got closer, I could see that the belly of the cow was hugely inflated, and that the cow was not moving and was, in fact, dead.

Back at the farmhouse, I told my friend, and she came out and we examined the cow more closely. There were no marks on her. Her legs didn't seem broken. My friend said she was one of the younger cows, so she hadn't died suddenly of old age.

"I'll investigate further," my friend said, as I was getting in my car to leave.

That night, she called me at the cabin.

"You'll never guess what killed that cow," she said.

"What?"

"Lightning."

There had been a storm the previous day and, apparently, there is a thing called "ground lightning," which is exactly what it sounds like—lightning that travels underground, erupting up out of the earth in low, damp spots. The cow had the misfortune to be standing in one of these low areas when the ground lightning sizzled beneath her hooves and electrocuted her. It is actually a very common killer of livestock and routinely takes out cows, often in multiple numbers. Afterwards, I read a story about a herd of nineteen cows in Texas who had all been killed by a single instance of ground lightning.

When I hung up with my friend, I sat with the puppies on the couch at the cabin. They were snoring away, and I was thinking about the randomness of everything—how the cow was literally in the wrong place at the wrong time; how I would never have seen it if the dogs hadn't tired themselves out on the trip to the river by bounding through the tall grass, so they couldn't walk in front of me on the way back; how quickly the trail had overgrown after I had spent days hacking through it, my arms stitched with blood from the sharp barbs of the prickly ash.

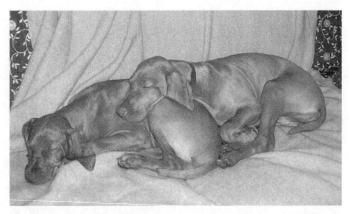
Violet and Charlotte at the cabin

EMILY DICKINSON WAS GIVEN her Newfoundland dog, Carlo, by her father, to be a companion for her on her rambles through the woods and fields around their home in Amherst, Massachusetts. In the eighteenth and nineteenth century, Newfoundland dogs were popular among the Romantics—Byron had one, as did Robert Burns, and Charles Dickens. Perhaps because of the literary connections, the breed was also popular in New England, and even the name, Carlo, was common, with five dogs in Amherst being registered under that name in 1858.[13]

Carlo lived to be an astonishing seventeen years old and accompanied Dickinson everywhere. She called him "My Shaggy Ally,"[14] and when he died, she did not replace him, preferring to think instead that he might be the one to greet her when she, in turn, died and went to heaven.

Carlo features in several poems, and the small tribute that Dickinson wrote for him when he died is not especially emotional. But, like Woolf, she sometimes mixed her own identity with that of her dog, once sending a lock of his hair in a letter to a friend, pretending that it was her own for a joke. She stated that dogs were better than human beings because they were capable of keeping secrets. She also believed that Carlo understood gravity because he knew to snap at the right place in the air to catch a morsel of cake that had fallen from a plate above him.

Even though Emily Dickinson didn't write much about her dog specifically, he was there in all her writing, because he was there for most of her walks, and walking,

"The Newfoundland Dog," an engraving by James Hope Stewart, c. 1834

for writers, is the fertile space where ideas are born, or phrases tried out and chosen.

The poet Mary Oliver wrote beautifully about both nature and dogs, and had many canine companions during her long life. She even wrote an entire book of poetry about dogs, called *Dog Songs,* in which she noted, "Because of the dog's joyfulness, our own is increased. It is no small gift."[15]

Mary Oliver
and Percy

Oliver lived most of her life in Provincetown, Massachusetts, where she walked daily in the woods and along the shore, usually accompanied by her dog, and wrote about what she encountered there.

The dog walk is not to be underestimated as a source for creativity and life-giving energy. Even if you take the same route every day, what crosses your path will always be different, and what the dog seeks out will lead you to discover new things. Increasingly, I have come to view my morning dog walk as the richest part of my day, and I often spend the hours after it thinking about what I saw or experienced on that walk. When I started a drawing practice last year, I collected bits of nature from the field and forest of the dog walk—twigs, acorns, milkweed pods, thistles, leaves—and made detailed drawings of these small entities, thus stretching the morning dog walk out even further. The desire to learn how to draw had come from observing the fields and forest. I can foresee a time, perhaps not that distant from now, when everything I make and think flows out of that two-hour walk every morning.

I remember an elderly friend of mine telling me with great authority that when you are young, you like the bright lights and excitement of a city, but when you get older, the excitement at the bird feeder is more than enough. I laughed at the time, but I can see that the dog walk might devolve into a similar kind of contentment for me.

When I moved with my then partner to the small town, Kingston, where I live, one of the first things we did was to seek out all the dog-walking spots. These have changed over the twenty-plus years I have been here—wasteland has been built on, public property has become private property—so it is necessary to always be on the lookout for new places where I can let a dog off leash, where there are trails and streams and patches of wood-land. The best places are the ones that have a variance of landscape—woods, water, some open fields, paths with elevation. They are even better if not many people know about them. There is nothing nicer than having the perfect spot to yourself, so I am prone to frequent these places early in the morning or just after dusk, when other walkers are at home.

While some of the walking locations have shifted, others have remained constant. My favourite local walk is the one I take every morning at a conservation area on the edge of the city. I know it as intimately as my dogs, have walked through it in all weather, and have seen many of its animal inhabitants. Experiencing it with the dog makes me aware of what else is there, and I pay attention to the landscape in a very immediate way, as my dog does.

Knowing this park as I do has made me think of how important setting is in a novel. Not so much what the setting is, but more what the characters know about it. What of a place is public, and what is private? What can be seen by everyone, and what is known only to a few people? My surroundings could be identical to my neighbour's surroundings, but if we are noticing different things about them, or using them in different ways, then we are actually living in different places from one another.

CHARLOTTE AND HER SISTER Violet were born in March, so they were young through the good weather. It is easier to introduce a dog to things in the summer, because all the outdoor activities are available. Hazel never liked water or swimming because by the time it was summer, she was almost a year old and not as flexible to new experiences as she had been when she was a puppy.

When the puppies were first in my care, I took them out to a friend's property outside of town, where they could wander freely over his ten acres. It was a hot day and his place was on the edge of a lake, so I decided to go swimming while I was there. I stripped down at the shore and plunged in, leaving the puppies on the bank and thinking they would stay there, would wait for me. But instead, they jumped into the water to follow me, bobbing around like little red corks, immediately good at swimming. They have liked swimming ever since. Charlotte used to hurl herself into the water near me if I was swimming, often landing almost on top of me. And if they were both in the water and you threw a stick for them, the dogs would swim back together, with both their mouths closed around the same stick.

Later that day, after the swim, we wandered over the property, then went to sit down outside the house and have a beer. Charlotte was tired and snoozed on the grass by my feet, but Violet went exploring and fell down a hill into a nest of fire ants. For the rest of the visit, she lay in my lap whimpering while I carefully picked all the biting red ants from her fat, tender belly, and Charlotte dozed blissfully on. This is how it became apparent, from the beginning, that Violet's life might be made harder because of her nature.

Having two puppies was overwhelming, but in my fog of grief, the feeling of being overwhelmed was actually good—not a distraction exactly, but a way of returning to the essentials of life. Like the puppies, I moved towards what felt good and away from what didn't. I operated primarily out of instinct and stopped doing many of the social things I had once done. The dogs were an excuse to get out of obligations that I could no longer bear, but they were also the reason for every day and I was grateful to them for that.

Because the grief over my brother's death, and Hazel's too, had forced me into a kind of continuous present, I couldn't stand to be inside any other moment than the one I was actually inside. So, writing fiction seemed a sudden impossibility. I didn't think that I could exist in the world of the novel at the same time as I was existing in my real life. Writing the memoir about my brother was possible because I wrote from the exact moment I was in, describing what the puppies were doing, or what noises I could hear through the walls of my house. It was the first time that I had put my real world into a book, and the experience of writing about my brother and myself, though a sad one, was also liberating because of this.

Near the end of the ten weeks when I had the two puppies full-time, we went for a walk to a conservation area just north of Kingston. There was a reservoir at one end of the conservation area, and I parked near there, where there would be fewer people to mind the dogs.

The puppies were over four months old, not small and stumpy anymore, but leggy and brimming over with energy. It was hard to keep them contained in any situation, but especially hard when there was a walk involved.

In the time it took for me to open the rear car door and fumble for their leashes, the dogs were out of the car and gone. I was only seconds behind them, but when I walked through the screen of trees that separated the car park from the reservoir, they were nowhere in sight.

I called—well, yelled for them and saw Violet coming through the grass towards me with what looked like an old grey boot in her mouth. It was a gosling, hanging limply from her jaws. She was pleased with herself and wagging her tail, but after more yelling, I was able to get her to drop the gosling, who immediately snapped back to life and scuttled away to safety. It had been a very good defence measure, to play dead, and I marvelled at the wisdom in it, and how instinctual it was. If the gosling had struggled, the dog probably would have killed it, but by going limp, it already seemed dead and the dog carried it gently because of this. (Vizslas are soft-mouthed dogs, meaning they don't clamp down on prey, but rather hold and carry it with minimal pressure.)

After clipping Violet onto her leash and making sure that the gosling was fine, I looked around for Charlotte and finally saw her swimming out into the middle of the reservoir after several adult geese.

The reservoir is large, more a lake than a pond, and it was a considerable distance to swim from shore to the centre of the basin. The geese were keeping just out of reach of the dog, and I know that this is a tactic they use to exhaust their predators, swimming just ahead of them until the predator eventually tires with the effort and drowns.

I yelled for Charlotte, but she kept on swimming, getting farther and farther away from shore, and from me.

I have never yelled so much as I do with the dogs. I don't, in fact, yell at any other time, but the kind of yelling I do with the dogs is almost always tinged with desperation because the dogs are often in mortal danger.

I stood at the edge of the reservoir, yelling, watching Charlotte's head get smaller and smaller as she went deeper out into the water in pursuit of the geese. And then something happened and the dog heard the desperation in my voice, or she remembered that she was attached to me, or she made a good decision for herself—whatever it was, she turned around and headed back. I was flooded with relief, as I have been many times since then when the dogs have done something that could have killed them but, miraculously, haven't died.

When I first went to pick up the puppies, the breeder said, casually, that they would probably have a strong prey drive because both of their parents were excellent hunters. I didn't really know what that meant at the time. Hazel, my previous vizsla, had had no interest in hunting. She sometimes half-heartedly went after a rabbit, but if she got close, she would stop chasing it and just watch it hop away.

Dogs with a high prey drive will go after something without regard for their personal safety. Hunting dogs regularly impale themselves on sticks from crashing through the woods after game, or break a leg from hurling themselves off a wall. I have wondered if it is perhaps the same feeling I have when I am writing well, which is a kind of crashing through the undergrowth, although far less dangerous.

Charlotte and Violet liked each other best when they

were hunting. Without a glance or a sound, they would begin to work a field in search of voles, or one of them would run in a looping circle after a squirrel, while the other dog ran a straight line to close the pursuit—the first dog forcing the quarry up into the path of the second dog. And while I never encouraged them to kill anything, I did like to watch them try—for their seamless telepathic communication and their pure joy in the chase.

The dog sisters got along best when they were out of doors. In the various doggy areas of the city, they were known collectively as the "Brontë sisters" because of their old-fashioned names. They were often together, indoors or out. Indoors, they scrapped for territory when they were young, and when they were old, they simply divided whatever space they were in, with Charlotte taking control of the downstairs of any given house, and Violet going upstairs. Even now that Charlotte has died, when Violet comes to my house, she goes to her usual spot upstairs and refuses to lie on the living room couch where her sister ruled the downstairs kingdom for almost a decade.

I think about the telepathy between the two vizsla sisters, and I often think too about non-verbal communication between dogs and humans. When you know a dog well, and they know you, much is understood between you. It's not telepathy but something else, some deep understanding that is perhaps the place that human language is always aimed towards but never really arrives at.

January 12

Freezing cold again this morning. I double-coated the puppy, but she was still cold and needed to be carried for a third of the walk. The winter wind was blowing sharp across the part of the park we call "the tundra," and she shivered in my arms and made me feel like a torturer for taking her out. It's hard to know what she will bear at this age, and I think I am often overestimating her abilities.

Saw a barred owl fly up from the ground, where it was hunting, to perch in a tree near the path. It swivelled its head right around to get a good look at the dog as we passed by. She didn't notice it, but she did see the squirrels in the woods and gave a sort of half-hearted chase to a couple of them.

In the evening, I went out to a movie with a friend and left the puppy in her crate for a few hours, the longest I have left her yet. She seemed fine when I got home, but the next day she was crazy, and I think that I probably left her in a bit too long and as a result her energy levels were high. The puppy is a fine-tuned machine and it seems impossible to get the formula right—how much time in the crate, how much time outside, how much time in play.

At puppy class this week, she was more adventurous. She wrestled a big sheepdog named Winston, who grew so excited that he shat on the floor, twice. Then one of the larger puppies attacked another dog, and when the instructor tried to break it up, she got bitten. She dripped so much blood on the floor that it had to be mopped up, even though she was quite relaxed about it! Puppy school is very dramatic.

Fig likes to watch the other dogs more than she likes to practise the commands. She is a good observer. Near the end of class, she climbed up on my lap and just watched the other dogs do their thing. She's as bad at school as I was, and does much the same thing that I did when I went—just observe everyone else.

She cried this morning and wanted me to cuddle her. I held her on my lap on the couch and she chewed at the end of my hoodie string, which seemed to make her feel better. Sometimes it's like she has existential angst and stands in the middle of the room crying or whining at nothing. Maybe she misses her family and it sometimes hits her that she is separated from them? I am learning that she is a dog with big emotions.

She is now too big for her cage in the car and the one in the house, but I haven't changed either of them out yet. She flops around like a fish inside them, trying to get comfortable. At night, I can hear her scratching and thrashing about. In the car, she can't sit up in the crate and has to crawl on her stomach to get inside. Once she's in, she's often reluctant to come out and has to be bribed with a biscuit.

It's funny, but I don't see her growing, and yet these things like the crates are indicators that she has grown. Her changes are measured by contrasting one time against another, rather than by my noticing her body growing. But when I look at her, I do notice that her legs are longer. Where once her head barely came up past my ankle, now it is level with my knee.

ANTON CHEKHOV HAD TWO DACHSHUNDS, named Bromide and Quinine, and called Brom and Khina for short. He described them in a letter to a friend thusly: "The dachshunds Brom and Khina are well. The former is dexterous and lithe, polite and sensitive. The latter is clumsy, fat, lazy and sly. . . . They both love to weep from an excess of feelings."

The dogs were his constant companions, and he would stage impromptu plays with them in the evenings to amuse his family. Dachshunds aren't easy dogs, and Brom and Khina were no exception. They were fierce guards of the property, terrorizing other dogs and the servants. As is common for their breed, they were diggers and regularly dug up the flower beds.

Anton Chekhov and Khina

Despite Chekhov's devotion to his dachshunds, his famous story "The Lady with the Dog" features a Pomeranian.

There is a bronze statue of Brom and Khina outside the former Chekhov house in Moscow. Visitors to the house rub the noses of the bronze dogs for luck. The noses have been rubbed so often that they are highly polished.

WHEN CHARLOTTE WAS about five months old, she and I were walking through the woods. We were on a well-worn trail and the dog was used to being off leash by then, and just trotted up ahead of me. It must have been a hot day, because I remember the cool of the trees, and the way the earthen path was dry and smooth like old leather. I also remember the loose-limbed gait of the young dog and how jaunty and confident her stride. It was always a joy to follow behind her, to have that exuberance lead me along countless trails.

We had just rounded a corner on the path, when up ahead of us, walking along the same trail, was a young stag.

Charlotte wasn't her adult hunting self yet, so she didn't give chase to the stag, and we all walked along together—the stag in front and us behind him—for at least a kilometre. It seems unlikely that the stag didn't know we were there, but he was obviously unconcerned by it. He was also young, like the dog, and had a similar loose gait. After a while, he simply stepped off the path back into the forest, and we kept walking past him. It was all very peaceful, and a little bit unreal, like we had wandered into a fairy tale. But this is something I have discovered about being out with the dogs. They are not wild creatures, yet I am often put in the way of wild things because of them. Almost all of my magical wilderness experiences have happened in their company. Once, I was walking with Charlotte in the woods and a young deer came bounding towards us. She had mistaken the vizsla for a deer because they look very much the same (a particular worry during hunting season). The expression on the deer's face was one of ecstatic joy and it was so wonderful to see it coming towards me rather than running away. Most of our human experience with wildlife is to stumble upon an animal and then watch as it quickly flees from us. But to see the naked joy on the young deer's face—an emotion that was so easy to read that it was a bit shocking—made me realize how narrow, and miserable, our encounters mostly are with wild creatures.

We used to walk a lot on the grounds of a former golf course on the edge of the city. The property had once been the city dump and garbage would sometimes surface in surprising ways on the course—a doll's arm reaching out of the earth on a putting green, the snout of an old bottle pushing up through a sand trap. Much of the land had grown over, but the big open fairway was still mowed and the dogs liked to race across it. Often we went there early in the morning or at twilight, when there was less chance of meeting anyone else.

When Charlotte and Violet were around three years old, I took them there at sunset, letting them off their leashes once we had exited the car park. There was no one else about and the dogs took off at full tilt across the fairway, then nosed around a scrubby hillock. The golf course bumped up on two sides to the river and into a kind of scraggly wood on the third side. The fourth side was the road. It was late fall and while there was still daylight in the trees, the light was leaving from the ground up and the grass was dark as water.

Far across the field, a shape started moving towards us. It was a coyote or coywolf—perhaps even that coywolf who we had first encountered when the dogs were puppies—huge and unafraid, coming towards the dogs to check them out.

Before I had a chance to yell, the dogs noticed the coywolf. Instead of coming towards me, they instantly gave chase, with all three disappearing into the little patch of woods.

Just as geese will lead a predator out into the middle of a lake or pond to drown them, so will a coyote or coywolf lead a dog into the underbrush where other members of their pack are waiting to rip them apart.

The coywolf was huge, about seventy or eighty pounds, much bigger than the fifty-pound weight of either dog. I screamed for Charlotte and Violet so desperately that I shredded my vocal chords, and for weeks afterwards, I could barely talk.

Violet came back within a few minutes, wagging her tail and seeming unconcerned, but Charlotte didn't return. Of the two dogs, Charlotte was the most confident, which tended to also make her the most stubborn. I kept yelling and moving towards the woods, but I couldn't cover ground like the dogs and by the time I could get in there, everything would have been over. But after ten minutes, when I had given up all hope, Charlotte trotted out of the woods, tail high, not a mark on her, and looking pleased with herself. Whatever had gone down in those woods, she had been the victor, not the victim.

January 13

Lots of snow fell in the night. The world was covered in fluffy white when we went for our morning walk. Fig has never experienced this much snow and it invigorated her.

She dashed through it and ate it off the ends of branches, snouted it off the path, and shook it vigorously off her back. I'm starting to really appreciate her zest for life, her desire to experience every little thing.

It was a beautiful walk. We saw two owls sitting in trees near the field, watching for voles. The sky was low and grey and the snow started falling again as we were walking back to the car. The walk lifted my spirits. It was so nice to see how happy Fig was made by the snow.

Fig has grown a bit too big for the car crate. I have to kind of stuff her in, and today she refused by stiffening her legs so that I couldn't push her under the lip of the cage door. I took her point and instead looped her leash around the headrest in the back seat. She sat up in the seat like a big dog, as good as anything, not seeming to need the crate at all anymore. I like that she knows what she wants and doesn't want, and that most of it seems very sensible.

Later that day, I had to go out to give a reading, and I left the dog with friends in my house. When I came home after a couple of hours, Fig collapsed in my arms when I sat down on the couch and she immediately fell asleep. I was told that she had run around like a maniac and then had howled at the door for me for a while. Her relief at seeing me was great and I could tell that she missed me when I was out. But it also made me aware that I don't want her to be unable to be with other people, to have separation anxiety from me, and that I need to make sure that I have her looked after by other people from time to time, to break total dependency on me. This is, however, not easy, as my friends are purposefully staying away because they don't appreciate the energy of the young puppy.

I have been letting Fig come upstairs sometimes, just to look around during the daytime. At night, I crate her in my bedroom and she doesn't have the chance to explore, but as she will eventually be allowed everywhere in the house, I thought it was a good idea to start letting her have a sense of what is up there.

She crawled onto my bed and rolled around in ecstasy, nosing through the mound of pillows, wriggling under the duvet. I think Charlotte might have already been in my bed at this stage, but Fig is still too bitey and squirmy to be a pleasant sleeping companion.

But her ecstasy at being on the bed confirmed what I noticed when I came home and she collapsed in my arms—she loves me now. I realize that I love her as well, and as with any time I have fallen in love, it seems both inevitable and a complete surprise.

ONCE, WHEN I WAS AT an arts colony, I was talking with another writer at dinner about dogs. She had Rhodesian ridgebacks, a breed that the vizsla is often mistaken for and vice versa. In our conversation, I mentioned that when Hazel was young, we had entered her in several dog shows, at the request of her breeder. In one show, she came second in her category, and in another show, she came third.

"What category was that?" asked the novelist.

"Sexually altered bitch."

The novelist laughed.

"Can I use that?" she asked.

I said yes, and a few years later, when reading her latest book, I came across the line about sexually altered bitches, and then a few years after that, a movie was made of the book and, on a long transatlantic flight, I watched it. That dog show line made it into the movie adaptation, and I remember the oddness of the feeling, hearing my line about my dog in a movie while I was hurtling through time and space in a tube above the ocean.

It pleased me that the novelist had enjoyed my line about Hazel's show career, and that all the gatekeepers on the film adaptation had also liked it enough to keep it in the movie. There is a sympathy between dog lovers, an understanding that we will find the same things amusing or touching about our dogs. If all else fails in a conversation, particularly when writers are forced to socialize with one another at a literary event, I know that if the person I am speaking with has a dog, we will never run out of things to say.

January 14

A bitterly cold day, but pretty with the snowfall. Took Fig for a short walk in the woods at the point when the day was the warmest, but she still shivered violently even with two jackets on. Vizslas have no undercoat, so they get cold very easily, and it seems that puppies can't regulate their temperature the way adults do, so I had to carry her back to the car at the end, and when we got home, she was still shaking. I wrapped her in a blanket and sat with her on the couch, but it took half an hour for her to get warm again, and I felt terrible for having taken her out. Her ears were freezing cold to the touch, which is a sign that she was too cold. There are fewer blood vessels in a dog's ears and in cold weather the dog diverts blood circulation from their ears to their internal organs.

There are such swings with the puppy—her energy shifts and mood changes, trying to determine if she will freeze outside or be energized by the outdoor activity. Balance seems impossible to strike in almost all of it, and I kind of lurch from mistake to success with very little indication of what any of my decisions will lead to.

I bought Fig a new crate and she seems to enjoy the extra space. It is wider than the previous one and she can move around more because of this. She almost slept right through the night last night because she was so comfortable in it.

Also, she is excellent in the car when she's not in a crate. I have stopped looping her leash around the headrest because if I was in an accident, she could strangle or have her neck broken. It is safer really to just have her loose until I can get a harness to use as a seat belt. She just sits in the back seat like a person, doesn't roam around the car, and when it warms up sufficiently, she lies down and goes to sleep. I am grateful that Fig is so good in the car. Some dogs get motion sickness, or pant and pace—all of which I would find very difficult.

We went to the vet for another set of shots and her first rabies vaccine. Fig likes the vet, but I've been through this before and know that everything changes after the spay. A dog that loved the vet before being spayed is afraid of the vet afterwards, or just tolerates visits there.

In the evening, we went to a friend's house for dinner and Fig tore around like a maniac, going up and down the stairs for no reason other than because she could, asking constantly to go outside and then immediately coming back in. She was very annoying, but then, just when she couldn't get more annoying, she fell asleep on the couch and looked very sweet. Walking home through the streets, she tried to go up every single driveway and every single flight of front steps, full of bluster and bravado and visiting energy.

January 15

Still very cold out, so no walking is possible. I took Fig to the car dealership when I went to get an oil change, and she was a big hit in the service area. In the showroom, she trotted around on her leash and sniffed all the tires of the new cars on display. Weirdly, there was a dog behaviourist in the waiting area. He tried to give me his card, but I declined, so he sat down beside me and proceeded to give me a lecture on dog training. He was an older man, slight, with lovely long lashes and false teeth. His hands were scarred, presumably from some of the dog training sessions that hadn't gone so well. It was lucky that Fig was, by fluke or exhaustion, behaving very well, sitting on the chair beside me, gnawing on her piece of fake rawhide. The behaviourist kept playing with her ears, which made her try to bite his hands. Then he tried to show me his method of bite inhibition, which is to press the dog's lips onto their teeth until they yelp and let go.

"But," I said, "it would work just as well if you stopped touching her ears while she's eating her bone."

No vizsla I have ever had has liked to be touched when they are doing something like eating, or when they are sleeping.

I was irritated by his endless chatter on how he trained dogs, when my dog was just minding her own business. As was I. He tried to give me his card again, but I declined.

This week at puppy class, Fig paid less attention than

usual. The instructors used her in a demo to show how to make a dog lie down, but she wouldn't co-operate and they couldn't make her lie down, even with a copious amount of dried liver bribes. What she really wanted to do was to play with the Irish setter called Peaches, and when she wasn't allowed to do this, she howled and was so over the edge with excitement and exhaustion that it was very hard to make her stop.

Winston shat again during playtime and the odour hung in the air for the remainder of the class. Fig likes playtime a thousand times more than she likes the training time. This week in playtime, she wrestled a German shepherd into submission and then stood over the prone dog in triumph for so long that the shepherd just went to sleep.

KAREN BLIXEN, who wrote under the name of Isak Dinesen, brought two Scottish deerhounds with her to Africa and continued to breed them while she was living there. She liked the deerhound for its hunting prowess, and also because they were historic dogs, having been featured in tapestries from ancient times, and she believed that they made any landscape they inhabited into an impromptu tapestry.

Her first deerhounds were a pair called Dawn and Dusk. Dawn had a relatively short life, as she was snatched from the porch of the Blixen farm by a leopard. Dusk, who was Blixen's favourite dog, lived much longer, but was eventually kicked to death by a zebra he was trying to kill.

Aside from the deerhounds, Blixen also had an antelope named Lulu living in her house that she had rescued as a fawn. The dogs, who hunted and killed practically everything else, left the antelope alone and respected her as a member of the household. Years after Lulu had been set free, she would sometimes appear at the open windows of the dining room at twilight, to have a look at her former family. Blixen was proud of this relationship and said in *Out of Africa*:

> It seemed to me that the free union between my house and the antelope was a rare, honourable thing. Lulu came in from the wild world to show that we were on good terms with it, and she made my house one with the African landscape, so that

nobody could tell where the one stopped and the other began.[16]

Karen Blixen and her deerhounds

WHAT DOES IT MEAN to know a place as a dog knows it? It is about knowing which bushes the rabbits are usually under, where the hole is in the fence that leads to a private field where once there was a deer killed by a coyote and where ever after it is worth checking out in case there is another carcass to savour. It is about knowing that chipmunks like to nest in the roots of the trees near the water, that not only birds will eat seed left in a woodland feeder but also wild turkeys, deer, and a plentitude of squirrels. In winter, there will be voles and mice under the frozen rind of the field grass. After a rain, the water in the puddles is sweet and preferable to the briny lake water for drinking.

After twenty-two years of following a dog through my morning park and seeing the world as she sees it, is there any place I know so well as that one? The dog's intimacy with the place has increased my own tenfold.

January 16

It was milder out today, and I triple-coated Fig's little frame, but she still shivered and became tired in the same spot on the walk and wanted to be carried. Instead of carrying her and continuing to walk, I just held her for a while and then put her down again and we continued on. We did this a couple of times, even sitting on a bench in one spot. Maybe this was the right kind of compromise, although I still think the walk is too long for her. So, perhaps I have to train myself in fits and starts and today was a beginning.

On the walk, we saw a barred owl in a tree at the edge

of the path, and then, when we turned the corner, the owl followed and perched on a tree near to us, clearly there to get a better look. I wonder if the owl was eyeing the dog and wondering whether to make a grab for her, or was simply curious about her or us? It was wonderful to have the opposite effect on a wild animal than the one we usually have, which is to scare the animal off.

There was a dozy winter fly in my house this morning, and Fig growled at it as it was crawling along the window ledge. When I swatted the fly, the puppy looked at me in alarm. Warning it off was one thing, but killing it was clearly another.

Another day, another half-eaten breakfast by Fig. When I mentioned to a friend the other day that Fig doesn't really like to eat, she said that she thought dogs liked either toys or food but were not usually motivated by or interested in both. This was true of Charlotte, who really had no interest in her toys, which is why they can still be used by Fig, as they are more or less in perfect shape.

One of the things I like to do while I am stuck inside with the dog is to look at the various online forums about vizsla puppies. I like to see what other puppies have done, or are doing, as a way to measure how Fig is progressing.

Mostly, reading the forums gives me a smug satisfaction that my dog, no matter how annoying, isn't as bad as some others. Thankfully, she is not biting me in the ass every time I turn around, or leaping up to counter height to snatch any food that is close to the edge, or barking non-stop when she is locked in her crate. But on the other end of this comparison, she has not mastered thirteen different commands, doesn't snuggle lovingly for hours, and isn't happily gulping down every meal and licking her bowl clean.

This morning, I bought chicken and some carrots, and I am going to boil them up and make a kind of mush to add to the new kibble and see if the puppy likes it any better. She looks thin to me, but not so thin that her tail-bones are visible. Her ribs can be seen but still have a bit of padding on them.

A few weeks ago, I came home late at night and when I drove into the laneway behind my house, where I park my car, there was a large rabbit trying to eat the last of the winter grass behind the fence. It is rare to see a rabbit in January and I admired its tenacity. Some of the carrots I bought today for the dog food, I put behind the house for the rabbit, in case it comes back.

January 17

Today was a sleety, rainy, miserable day. We went for a short walk in the woods. Fig pawed at my legs, wanting me to carry her over the puddles of slush. I did, and then didn't. She's getting heavier every day it seems, also taller and longer, and it's a struggle to heft her up into my arms. Last week, she could run under the coffee table. This week, she bangs her head on it when she tries. And where she once wriggled easily under the couch, now she gets stuck and moans with frustration, emerging all snappy and irritated.

Most of Charlotte's old toys have been destroyed. Fig likes to bite the face off the stuffed animals and then slowly and lovingly extract all the fluff that fills up the body of the bear or wolf or hedgehog. All my pockets are full of this fluff, wrestled out of the dog's mouth, but she has probably eaten as much as I have recovered. I can see wisps of it poking out of her poo in the yard.

There's a natural mayhem to this puppy that I am slowly getting used to. She dashes around the house in a frenzy, chews the face off a stuffie, barks at the fireplace poker, tries to crawl under a piece of furniture she's out-grown, growls at her reflection in the window, bats a bug across the kitchen floor, gnaws energetically on a bone, and then collapses in a heap and sleeps for an hour. Then she gets up and does it all again.

This afternoon, I heard what seemed like a familiar voice outside my house and looked out to see the dog trainer that I had met at the car dealership, walking the neighbour's dog stiffly up and down the street with the neighbours watching. Fig sat up on the couch and followed their movements from inside the house, curious as to why the dog was simply going back and forth in front of our window.

January 18

There's been a change in Fig on the morning walk. She is no longer so focused on me and her attention has turned to the larger world. She sniffs a branch, eats a piece of ice, carries a pine cone around for a while, lurches after a squirrel. She has started behaving like a big dog. And now in the car, on the drive over, she is large enough to sit and look out the window.

The recent bitter cold has made it hard to give the dog the outside exercise she requires. She has a lot of energy that is hard to burn off as a result. One of the things I worry about, especially in winter when the surfaces are treacherous, is that something will happen to me and there will be no one to manage her considerable puppy demands. A common worry of parents, I know, but the new, young dog is making me feel my age like nothing else has thus far. I am more cautious and careful than usual on the ice, or when doing something simple like bringing in firewood or shovelling the walk. Her well-being depends on my well-being, and I have to make sure that nothing happens to me. At night, I lie in bed and listen to the squish and lurch of my heart, hoping it has the strength to survive the next decade with an energetic vizsla. I had thought that having a puppy again might keep me young, but it is having the opposite effect and making me feel old.

This morning, when I struggled Fig into her coat, she grabbed one of my shoes and held it in her mouth while I dressed her. And because she had something in her mouth, she was compliant and didn't bite. I can't believe I didn't think of this before and have been fighting her this whole time when instead I could have just let her hold something in her mouth and make the whole enterprise much easier. Another example of the way a dog tells us what to do with them, and if we're paying attention and not fixated on having our way, by listening to what they're trying to communicate, we could get along with them better. This is not dissimilar to writing, where it is more effective to listen to intuition instead of trying to force your will upon a piece of work.

The walk this morning was our first walk with Violet, who is now almost ten years old and a bit grouchy with other dogs, especially puppies. But after a little initial snarling, which made Fig keep her distance from the older dog, Violet just ignored the puppy and we had a nice, albeit icy, stroll through the woods. It was strange seeing Violet so old now and Fig so young, like some weird kind of time travel. The sight of the puppy brought me back to the time when Charlotte and Violet were little puppies themselves. I wondered what Violet felt, what she remembers of her sister. At one point in the walk, she ran with Fig, the two of them side by side, the way she used to run with Charlotte.

Because I once spent so much time with Violet, as she was often with Charlotte, I don't want her to feel abandoned by me. Once a week now, on Tuesday afternoons, I take her to the woods by herself and she bounces through the trees and I collect dry sticks from the trees or the forest floor to use as kindling for my fireplace. It is always nice to be with Violet again, in a way that we're both so used to. All the old familiarity comes rushing back within the first few steps of our walk.

THE ENGLISH POET ALEXANDER POPE suffered from a form of tuberculosis that enfeebled him and stunted his growth. Less than five feet in height, he feared for his safety in the dangerous London of the eighteenth century, so he bought an enormous Great Dane to protect him. He called the female dog Bounce, and every day he went out with the dog and two loaded pistols into the streets of the city. Bounce protected him outside and inside his home, once attacking and subduing a male servant who was attempting to kill and rob Pope.

When Bounce had a litter of puppies, Pope gave one of them to his friend the Prince of Wales, with a collar for the dog on which was engraved the couplet: "I am his Highness' dog at Kew; / Pray tell me, sir, whose dog are you?"

Alexander Pope and his dog Bounce

Bounce died while in the care of one of Pope's friends, and Pope was quick to follow, dying less than two months later.

January 19

This morning, there was blood on the path through the woods and two dead voles on the snow. We saw the barred owl and met a photographer who had taken a photo of the great horned owl that is apparently in the area. He also said that he has seen numerous coyotes in the park and that last week, he and a friend saw a wolf.

"A wolf?" I asked, thinking that he was mistaking a

coyote for a wolf, but he insisted that he knew the difference and maintained that there was a wolf in the park.

Fig is now testing my authority by not coming back every time I call her, even though she usually doesn't go more than twenty feet ahead of me. But she is still so small and it would be easy for a predator to snatch her off the path.

Took Fig to a friend's house last night and tried to keep her on the leash while we ate supper, as a substitute for the crate. She resisted strongly for a while, thrashing around on the end of the leash like a fish on a line, but eventually, reluctantly, she settled down on a blanket beside my chair to chew on a bone. Where Charlotte would have just acquiesced, Fig has to fight, and I can see that this is part of her nature. She will not necessarily be an easy dog, but she has a boldness that might mean she is a fairly fearless dog, which is its own kind of ease. Still, I anticipate how her resisting me, if it continues past the puppy stage, will get tiresome.

January 20

On the walk this morning, there was fresh blood on the snow and we saw two owls lifting off the ground and into the trees. Lots of hunting going on. Winter is a hungry time in the woods.

Fig doesn't have good control of her back legs yet and uses them as a unit, like a rabbit. She hops about and the back legs thump up and down and don't operate independently yet.

After the walk, I stopped to buy some groceries, leaving Fig in the back seat of the car. So far, she has been very good in the car and stays put in the back seat, but when I came out of the shop, I found her on the floor in the front seat, underneath the pedals. She is obviously testing the limits of her world in every instance, which, I suppose, means she feels confident enough to push past the boundaries.

In the park, I met someone who had known Charlotte and she commented on how hard it must be to get another dog after I had loved Charlotte so much. I didn't say it, but I thought what a strange comment that was, really. If you have loved someone or something, why wouldn't you want to love again? To not have another dog to love would feel like the difficult thing.

I remember when Charlotte was a puppy and I was strolling with her through a city park and a woman ran up to me in her nightdress. She had seen me walking the dog from her third-floor apartment. Her own dog had died the day before and that dog had looked like Charlotte, and the woman couldn't stop herself from running down three flights of stairs and across the early morning grass towards a dog that so resembled her own. This is how much she had loved her dog, that she had no regard for her appearance, or her actions, that she couldn't help herself or stop herself from launching out of her grief towards Charlotte. It was a beautiful, wild moment, made even more so by her kneeling on the grass beside my dog and throwing her arms around her neck.

"I thought he'd come back," she said.

PACING

B efore my brother died, I had been working on a novel about the writer and critic Charles Sainte-Beuve, who was a friend of Victor Hugo and was, briefly, Adèle Hugo's lover. The novel came out in the fall after Martin's death, and when I toured for the book, I wrote about events on the book tour in the long letter I was penning to my brother that became the memoir *Nocturne*. One of the most heartbreaking things was reading from *The Reinvention of Love* on Granville Island for the Vancouver Writers Fest in a theatre next door to the music school where my brother had played the piano every week as one of his jobs. The last time he played the piano, in fact, was at that music school.

Grief moves at its own pace and there isn't much one can do to speed it up. I was learning just to move with it. With the advent of the new dogs, I had been paying attention to the animals and birds I saw every day, noting what crossed my path. Not as a way to make specific meaning out of a particular creature, but more to see what was keeping my sorrow company on any given day. On the book tour, in Banff, I was walking back up the hill to the Banff Centre, and as I passed a wooded area, I looked in and saw a great grey owl sitting on a stump in a clearing in the forest. The owl noticed me and swooped up out of the woods, huge grey wings stiff as sails. These flashes of wildlife were always exhilarating, seen with dogs or without.

The first year with a dog is intense because the puppy needs to be exposed to all the elements that will compose her life. If she is going to travel in a car, she needs to do this when she is still young, so she won't be afraid. She needs to be taken into crowded places, so she won't be afraid of crowds, exposed to noise, so she won't recoil or run when she hears a gunshot or car backfire.

When Charlotte was six months old, I took her on her first canoe trip. My previous dog, Hazel, was very good in a canoe and an adept camping companion, and

I needed Charlotte to have the same abilities, because in the summer, I like to go canoeing. I always felt very smug when canoeing with Hazel, as she would sit motionless in front of me, or lie with her head resting on the thwart. Often, we passed other canoeists with dogs who weren't nearly as good in the boat—dogs who lumbered from side to side, almost tipping the canoe and eliciting panicked yells from their people.

Charlotte and I went on the canoe trip with a friend who I had gone on many trips with in previous years. On one particularly memorable trip, which Hazel was on, it rained continuously day and night for the entirety of our five-day journey. We wore rain gear the entire time, and covered the dog in the boat with a tarp when we were paddling. Each day we broke camp and canoed to a new site, often portaging up steep hills, which in the rain became mudslides. It rained so hard sometimes that we just had to stand still, with heads bent, letting the rain pour off us, and give Hazel shelter under the overturned canoe while we waited for it to let up so that we could continue our portage. At each new camp, we would first put up a tarp, then erect our tents beneath it, reversing the process when we broke camp. In this way, we stayed dry, but it was a hard trip and fairly joyless. I remember the relief with which Hazel dove into the tent to burrow into a sleeping bag the moment the tent went up.

On Charlotte's first canoe trip, there was no rain in the forecast. Our challenge was that my friend was expected at a wedding on the morning of the day we would paddle out. We were going three lakes deep into the park, so this meant that we would have to break camp in the middle of the night and portage and paddle out in the dark.

We had chosen a trip where the dog wouldn't have to spend too long in the canoe, because it is hard for a vizsla puppy to be still. So, we paddled one lake that took about an hour, then walked over a half-hour portage, where the dog could race back and forth. Then we paddled another lake that was slightly longer, and walked across another portage that was also slightly longer. We camped on the third lake.

Charlotte was good on the trip, not wandering away, sitting between my legs in the back of the canoe. She liked sleeping in the tent, and we spent a nice couple of days together, with not a single drop of rain.

On the night we had to leave, we went to bed around nine and woke up at three, using our headlamps to pack away the camp. The dog was confused as to why there was so much activity in the middle of the night, but she stayed close and I had to trust that she would, because I couldn't leash her when there was so much to carry and put away that I didn't have a free hand to hold on to her.

I had thought that it would be scary to walk back over the portages in the dark, but it was so peaceful and quiet, and not scary at all. The lakes were still and there was a tiny strip of moon and lots of stars. It was thrilling being the only humans out there. Charlotte was good, taking the work seriously, walking back and forth with us across the portage as we ferried the canoe and the gear from one end to the other. I had a pocket full of dog biscuits to bribe her along, but I didn't need them. She enjoyed the dark walk as much as we did, and when we hit the final lake, the dawn was breaking and we paddled into the sunrise, with the mist rising around us and all three of us quiet with the wonder and beauty of the new morning.

Charlotte was the dog of mine who operated at the same frequency as me. We didn't have similar natures, but our natures worked together. We kept pace with one another, and maybe that's what it was, that we simply moved at the same speed through our days.

THE POPULAR CHILDREN'S writer Margaret Wise Brown was a "beagler," which meant that she hunted with beagles in a pack after rabbits or hares. Unlike fox hunters, who travel mounted on horseback, beaglers are on foot, following the pack of hounds as they chase down their quarry. Brown, who had been an athlete in college, was so fast that she could keep pace with the dogs and would crash through the undergrowth with them in their pursuit, while the other beaglers took easier, less painful routes around the bushes and trees in their path.

Brown was one with the dogs, not distant or different from them in their excitement at the hunt. I have run like this with Hazel, so know what this experience feels like. I like to think that the exhilarated rush is similar to how writing feels when it is going well.

Knowing this about Brown gives new meaning to the title of one of her famous children's books, *The Runaway Bunny*. Also interesting is the fact that she wrote her most popular book, *Goodnight Moon*, as a homage to her literary hero, Gertrude Stein, using some of the experimental writer's rhyme schemes. Her last book, *Mister Dog: The Dog Who Belonged to Himself*, was inspired by her pet terrier, Crispin's Crispian.

Brown died at the age of forty-two from a blood clot following a simple operation. She was demonstrating to the nurses that she was in fine fettle, kicking up her heels to show them and dislodging a blood clot in her leg that then travelled to her heart, killing her instantly.

Margaret Wise Brown and Crispin's Crispian

Brown was naturally athletic, and so her inclination to run to hounds with her dogs was perhaps an extension of her personality. But other writers do not start out being so physically active and are instead helped in that direction by their dogs.

PACING IN A BOOK is what moves the story along. In poetry, I learned that a line will carry the rhythm of the body and will break where the poet takes a breath. Prose doesn't have the same parameters as poetry, but I believe that its lines also echo the rhythm of the writer and that the metre of the prose holds within it the breath and heartbeat of the writer. That becomes the natural pacing of a story, and sometimes that is adequate, just to go with how a narrative moves organically. Sometimes, though, it is necessary to manipulate the prose, to alter the pacing. If a story is without much action or drama, a writer can speed up the pacing to give the narrative more tension and urgency, to literally make it go faster. This is done by shortening the sentences, chopping things up, rushing the rhythm along. This can also be done by cutting out some of the linkages. A writer once told me to delete every third sentence, as this will remove some of the natural transitions and enliven the language. Though it seems an odd thing to do, it actually works surprisingly well.

January 22

Violet and I went on our Tuesday afternoon walk. It was finally sunny out and relatively warm, so we did a little woodsy loop along the lakefront. On the drive there, I passed a field where I have discovered a female snowy owl is in winter residence. She sits up on the chain-link fence around the baseball diamond, and I have gone to look at her there every day for a week. I mean to go there one day at dusk and watch her hunt over the sports field.

The beautiful thing about walking with Violet is that I can open the car door and let her out and she will race through the woods, chasing squirrels, and I can stroll along at a leisurely pace, and we don't have to really have any contact with each other until we are both back at the car. I know this dog so well, and she is ten years old now, so less likely to want to court trouble. Being with her is a comfortable experience for me. There were so many times when Charlotte and Violet and I walked together. It is so different than walking with the puppy, where I have to constantly be on alert for her antics or bad decisions.

At puppy class tonight, I had to leave halfway through for a previous commitment, but really, this was precisely at the point that Fig and I tire of the class anyway, so it was not a sacrifice. Fig seems to have mastered "down" without my having really practised with her. She was ter- rible at "off" in class, but when I tried it with her later in my kitchen, she was good at it. The other puppies are a distraction to learning, but the socialization aspect of the class is good, which I guess is the whole point of it anyway.

On the way out at break, we passed Winston having a shit outdoors for a change.

Here's something I wonder: If a puppy is born in winter, is young in winter, does she know instinctively that there will be a spring and summer to come, or will it be a complete surprise?

A FAST PACE IN A STORY will move that story along at a clip and move the reader with it. Murder mystery writers are usually very good at pacing, knowing what to portion out when. Agatha Christie moved her prose at a good clip through her many books. Christie also had a love of dogs all of her life, from her first dog, a mongrel terrier called George Washington, to her last dog, the Manchester terrier Bingo, who was renowned for biting everyone.

Her favourite dog was a wire-haired terrier named Peter, who was with Christie when her first husband left, and her mother died, and after her breakdown and disappearance to Harrogate. He was also the model for "Bob," who stars in her book *Dumb Witness*, about a murder that is disguised as an accident involving a dog's ball lying at the top of a staircase. The book is dedicated to Peter, who is called "A dog in a thousand."[17]

It seems no accident that Christie's favourite dog came at a difficult time in her life, as it seems no accident that my favourite dog also came at a difficult time. Perhaps

Agatha Christie and Peter

during these moments of death and hardship, we are more open and vulnerable than at other, smoother times, and therefore we are capable of feeling more and deeper, and it makes sense that the attachment to the dog that goes through this time with us is correspondingly great.

When Charlotte was young and lying on my bed, I went to move her and she growled at me. There are trainers who would say that I should have immediately removed her from the bed and made her lie on the floor, shown her who was "boss," and made her subservient. But I don't believe in that way of doing things. I believe that a dog needs to have good manners, as people do, because this makes it easier for them to negotiate the world and for the world to tolerate them, but I don't want to dominate a dog. I want instead to work with who they are. So, when Charlotte growled at me, I distracted her by showing her a toy, and she stopped. Then I coaxed her off the bed with that same toy. I didn't make anything of her behaviour, so that she wouldn't get attached to it and believe it was something she should do again. Dogs will get fixed very quickly on what has been effective. So, if Charlotte growled at me and I was afraid and backed off, she would use the behaviour again, and soon it would be her set way of operating and it would be very hard to convince her out of it.

As I came to know Charlotte, I learned that she was a brave dog, a dog with a great deal of pride in her ability to stand up for herself. Confronting a dog like her wasn't the best way to stop her from doing something, because she wouldn't back down. It was better to approach her in a sort of sideways manner.

I learned to read her body language. If she stiffened or had sudden acute focus, it meant she was stiffening

into a more fight type behaviour—like territorial growling, or snapping at another dog she didn't like. If you
challenged her directly, she would just stand her ground,
but she could always be moved sideways by distraction
and could be persuaded out of her assertive behaviour
quite easily. Over time, as she became more comfortable
with herself and her surroundings, she let a lot of those
behaviours go, and rarely went into her stiffening mode
and never growled at anyone.

I admired her character and her bravery. Her habit of
not backing down from anyone or anything created some
problems in her life and mine—she was sprayed twice by
a skunk and quilled three times by a porcupine, for example—but it could also be depended on. I knew that she
would defend me to the death, if necessary. She was not
afraid. She stepped into the breach and always moved
towards things, not away from them. I never worried
about anything when I was with her, because I knew that,
no matter what crossed our path, she would take care of it.

Her bravery made her confident, and I saw her win a
fight with a dog once from her confidence alone. The fight
was not one she had wanted or started, but when she was
attacked, she stood her ground. I thought she was going

to be killed because the other dog was both younger and stronger, but there was a moment in the fight when the other dog lost confidence. I could see it happen. It was a faltering, and in that faltering, Charlotte moved forward swiftly, chasing the younger dog away with her tail between her legs.

When Charlotte was young, I took her to see a friend of mine who breeds dogs and, after an afternoon together, my friend told me that I had an "aloof" dog and that these were the best kind of dogs, because they were independent, had autonomy, operated almost entirely out of their own instincts, and usually had very good common sense.

Even at the end, when Charlotte developed a swift and sudden cancer in her heart and I had to have her euthanized, when the vet came to the house and wanted to sedate the dog before giving her the heart-stopping needle, I said it wasn't necessary.

"She will want to know what is happening," I said. "And she won't give you any trouble."

The vet didn't, or wouldn't, believe this and gave Charlotte the sedative anyway, because this is what she usually did, how this procedure worked. But Charlotte wasn't sedated, wouldn't close her eyes. She was awake and unafraid for her own death, faced it head on, with all the courage with which she faced everything in life.

When I miss her now, one of the things I miss the most is her boldness, and her courage in moving forward, towards whatever was in her path, even death.

Charlotte

January 24

Fig is suddenly much bigger, and with her changes in size have come a few other subtler changes. She is still a biter, but she is biting less and I can actually touch her now without her going for my hand. Now when she throws herself on me in the mornings to cuddle before our walk, she is so big that her head thunks against the wall behind me. She has not adjusted to her new size and crashes into a chair, thinking she can slide under it. She almost brains herself a dozen times a day, but she just shakes her head and continues on. Puppies are very resilient.

Each new change erases the previous one. I wonder if she is confused by her growing body in the way I was confused by mine when I was young?

There was a blizzard today, so it was hard to walk the dog. As a result, she had a lot of energy and was a maniac in the house. She bit my lip and drew blood, chewed on the fireplace logs and ate bits of the wood, even with repeated efforts from me to make her stop. She also tore around at top speed, wanted out and then in again, emptied the box of toys and bones—which is actually my grandmother's old Sussex trug basket that she once used for gardening. And now, Fig, worn out by her craziness, is sleeping beside me, also worn out by her craziness.

It seems that the growth spurt coincides with a spike in bad behaviour. I wonder if it feels bad to grow so quickly? Does it hurt? How strange to be in a body that will fit under the coffee table one day and not the next. What does she make of the changes that are happening to her?

After tiring of Fig's boundless energy in the house, I bundled her into three coats and took her for a little walk off leash in the park until her feet became too cold for her to continue. She will now sit nicely for me to put her collar on, but she still thrashes and struggles and bites when I attempt to put on the layers of protective clothing. She particularly loathes the sweater that I have to pull over her head. This is a definite disadvantage of having a winter puppy—having to dress them for winter.

The breeder has used Fig's photo to advertise his dogs, so I guess that means she is a fine example. On his website are testimonials from other owners, and I read through some of them today. Most of the dogs are described as "intelligent," "gentle," "cheerful," and also "not backing down, even with bigger dogs." All of these descriptors seem to apply to Fig, and I wonder how much of what I am thinking is her personality has been bred into her bloodline?

Rain and snow this afternoon, so I took Fig to one of the Puppy Play hours at the dog school. This time, we met an enormous five-month-old Labradoodle there named Huggy, who probably weighed sixty-five pounds. He became aggressive quickly, and because he was so enormous and could easily overpower, and possibly hurt, Fig, they only "played" together for about five minutes. The barricade went up and he went on one side and played with a pit bull puppy who showed up late, and Fig stayed with me and ran around after a ball. Huggy's owner is a woman older than me, who has absolutely no control over her dog at all. She carries a spray bottle filled with vinegar everywhere and told the trainer that she has to leash the dog even in the house or else she can't make him do anything. Having control over one's dog only works if the dog is agreeing with this notion. Some dogs simply don't want to listen or obey, and if they are large and powerful like Huggy, it could be difficult to make them do what is wanted. I have never been a very big disciplinarian with my dogs, but they have always had some kind of desire to please me, so we have been able to eventually meet on a middle ground.

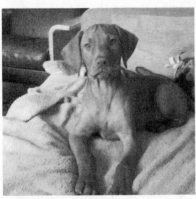

Fig at eleven weeks

We have our last puppy class tomorrow night, and I don't think I will take Fig back for part two of the puppy program, called "Puppy Graduate." She learns better just doing a bit of training everyday with me and not being distracted by a room full of other dogs. And she plays better with my partner's dog than with any of the "puppies," most of whom have been disappointing in one way or another. All I want from Fig is that she come when called, walk reasonably on a leash, and lie down on command and stay down if I am at a café or a reading and need her to be still and quiet. I think we can probably master these things together and save the puppy school money.

I find myself wondering at the whole obedience thing. How much will a dog naturally do for you if they are bonded with you? How much is just dependent on their good natures and level of attachment to you? I'm feeling that the attachment is the important thing at the moment and that perhaps the most vital things I am doing with Fig is not obedience work, but the time we spend snuggling together on the couch. So, to this end, I did not crate her for the entire day and just let her roam around and sleep on me. It was hard to get any work done, but I could type a bit with one hand while she slept on me. I think it did her good to be out of her crate all day, and I think that it made the bond between us stronger. It shouldn't surprise me to learn that everything really is all about love.

THE CRAZINESS OF THE PUPPY BRAIN is nowhere more in evidence than when Fig plays with a toy called Bob-a-Lot. This is a featureless plastic treat dispenser that wobbles around the floor, releasing bits of dried liver or other treats out of a little door at the base of the weighted bulb. The idea is that the dog pushes at the Bob-a-Lot with her nose or paws, and after a few smacks or nudges, the movement will drop a treat down to the opening. It is meant to be mentally stimulating and keep a dog entertained for hours.

A friend of mine gave Fig one of these as a present, and when I first showed it to her, she was scared by the lurching movement of the toy and didn't want to go near it. After I had demonstrated what could happen if she did approach it, by batting it around the floor myself until it released its treasures, Fig showed more interest in it. Now she is obsessed with Bob-a-Lot. The moment she sees me reach for it on the shelf, she jumps up and utters a high-pitched shriek. When it is on the floor, she barks shrilly at it if it doesn't dispense the treats fast enough, eventually losing her temper altogether and trying to bite the smooth, rounded sides or gnaw at the little trapdoor in a fury.

I can see, from her responses to Bob-a-Lot, how little control Fig has over her emotions. She can't regulate anything about herself—her feelings, her temperature, her growing body. She has no patience, no attention span, and no understanding of what is happening to her when she suddenly gains an inch or her gums start bleeding from the first nubs of her adult teeth. Her world is so small— she is only twelve weeks old and has only been alive for one season—and yet it is shifting constantly in catastrophic ways. No wonder she is often furious! I can understand her frustration with Bob-a-Lot, although I also think I will have to ration her interactions with the toy.

BEING A WRITER is confusing because it is both lonely and all-consuming. It is no surprise to me that writers often suffer from mental health issues or substance abuse issues, or even kill themselves. It is hard to stay healthy in a profession that has so much instability and failure built into it. It is hard to remain in the state of vulnerability necessary for creation, while also handling the demands of life and making a living, and dealing with all the rejection that is standard fare. There is always rejection in a writer's life, whether for a grant, or a prize, or being turned down by a publisher. It never ends. Sometimes the loneliness is the easier part.

If one is set on a writer's life, it is a good idea to be able to pace yourself—to not work too hard or too much, to make sure you have enough physical and social activity, to try and cultivate healthy habits. A dog helps make all of this easier.

A dog comes into a room with you and sits by your chair or lies at your feet. A dog nudges you to go out for a walk or throw a ball down the hallway. A dog demands attention from you in a way that doesn't feel like a demand, but more like a relief. The concentration needed for writing means that it is difficult to have other people in the same room with you when you are writing, in case they interrupt. A dog is often the only being allowed in the same room with a writer, and this makes a world of difference to the writer's loneliness.

The kind of intimacy that a dog offers is perhaps ideal

for a writer, because intimacy with other humans often takes the writer away from their work, while intimacy with a dog brings the writer closer to their work.

The most intimate relationship with a dog that I had was with Charlotte. Our particular chemistry, whatever it was, worked for the both of us and made our companionship easy and deeply satisfying. While I don't think that Charlotte considered I had authority over her, she did have respect for me. She let me walk through the door first. She would never touch anything of a food nature that I had left with her in the car. Once, I left an entire ham on the front seat of the car for an hour while she was in the back seat and I was off doing various errands. When I returned to the car, the dog was lying in her spot and the ham was untouched. She would never even venture into the front seat of the car, but always kept to her designated space in the back. She had good manners and would follow my lead.

But if she felt that another dog or person was more or less at the same level as her, in whatever hierarchy she operated under, then she would have no qualms about taking what was theirs. This included not only her sister but unfortunately also my partner, who once left a wrapped sandwich on the front seat of the car and came back to find that Charlotte had delicately unwrapped the cellophane and then eaten the entire sandwich. In the dog's mind, my partner and she were equals, and all was fair between equals.

If I had been away for a while, Charlotte would press her head into me and breathe me in with great inhalations. When she wanted something from me—a biscuit or to drink the foam from my coffee at the bottom of the cup—she would put her paw lightly on my shoulder, like a benediction. If she received a present from someone, she made sure to greet that person at the door whenever they visited, holding their gift in her mouth. So, my partner was greeted with the spotted dog she had once given Charlotte, and my mother, the large, brown bear. The neighbours two doors down were always presented with the stuffed mallard they had once given to the dog.

When my partner's small dog, whom Charlotte had tolerated but never really liked, died, and my partner came to our house for the first time after the death, Charlotte went to where my partner was sitting on the couch and put her paw on Nancy's chest, right above her heart. She then lowered her head until it was touching Nancy's forehead and kept it there for a long while. It was impossible to mistake the gesture as anything other than sympathy and compassion.

She was a dog of deep feeling and a dog who believed in maintaining order. When a friend's dog was swimming after a beaver across a river and ignoring all of our cries to return to shore, Charlotte jumped in the river and swam after him, barking at him until he turned around and followed her back to shore. If her sister was being unruly, Charlotte would discipline her by running at her and barking in her face. Once, I was in a park in Toronto and a woman was trying to get her out-of-control dog to calm down—the dog was running in circles around her and jumping on her. Charlotte went over and scruffed the dog to bring him into line, so that he stopped his bad behaviour and sat politely down beside his person.

She had a strong sense of how things should be, and she wasn't shy about making sure everything, and everybody, was in its proper place. She would have done well managing a dormitory, with her sense of fairness and her gentle but insistent style of discipline.

Whenever I was stressed or upset, she would press against me and offer me her belly to be rubbed, to take my mind off my troubles—and also because she liked to have her belly rubbed and this was a good opportunity to get me to rub it—she was nothing if not pragmatic.

What I think about now that she's gone is how well we knew each other. So much could pass between us with a glance. I could tell, from the slightest change in her posture, what she was feeling, and vice versa. And here's the thing I realize fully now: the dog saved me, kept me going.

When Charlotte was dying and stopped eating, she did it gradually. First, she refused her kibble and the wet food that sometimes accompanied it. Then she wouldn't eat peanut butter. Then toast. Next ice cream, which we tried to bribe her with, and then her beloved slices of Mennonite sausage, which had always been a fail-safe choice. But cheese, however, went right to the end. On her deathbed, when all other food was snubbed, she would still accept and gobble a sliver of four-year-old local cheddar.

The cancerous tumour that was in Charlotte's heart caused the sac that surrounded that organ to fill with blood. Left alone, undetected, the sac would have burst and the dog would have suffered a painful death. Luckily—if discovering something fatal can be considered lucky—I had taken her to the emergency vet on a Sunday evening in July because she was clearly uncomfortable. An X-ray revealed the enlarged heart sac, and so we made a late-night drive to the emergency pet hospital in a neighbouring city to have the blood drained by needle aspiration from the sac. There was no cure for the tumour, but draining the sac would give us some extra minutes, hours, or days, before it filled up again. At that point, the dog would have to be euthanized.

We got an extra day from the procedure. An entire extra day, which I was very grateful to have, and which felt monumental in scope. It was a beautiful day and we rose early in the morning and went walking with a friend, as we had done for pretty much every morning since we were first together.

The place where we liked to walk is a little piece of wilderness close to the city. There are fields and woods and water, and often wildlife to spot. On this particular morning, Charlotte jumped out of the car and immediately started hunting for voles—which was her favourite activity—in the field that bordered the car park. She was hunting with intensity, and it seemed to me that she was really focusing in on what gave her pleasure, what made her feel like herself, and disregarding everything else.

And right at the beginning of that walk, it all felt a bit magical. There were birds all around us, spinning through the air above our heads—cardinals, woodpeckers, finches—in a wheel of colour and song.

Later on, in the woods, we met all the people whom Charlotte liked to meet—the ones who gave her biscuits and made a fuss over her—and there were rabbits and squirrels to lunge after (although not chase, because she didn't have the energy). Coming through the last field, my companion gave the dog a piece of toast, and Charlotte took it as a prize and carried it proudly all the way back to the car. She wasn't interested in eating it but in taking it as her prey, which was another way of feeling good about herself. And there, in the last field, we saw three stags, walking slowly along, not twenty feet from us. This was something that, in all our years of coming to this place, we had never seen before. It felt connected to the dog and to her imminent death, and I remembered the stag that Charlotte and I had walked behind when she was young. And here we were again, walking beside the stags, the dog carrying her toast, her tail high. It seemed such a celebration, to have the stags as escorts to usher my dog out of this world. It was beautiful and moving, and here is another thing that strikes me now: how many of the truly beautiful things I have experienced have been because of, or with, my dog.

The stag, in many mythologies, is the link between this world and the next and belongs to this "thin place" between worlds.

On the way home in the car, I opened the rear window fully and Charlotte stuck her head out and breathed in great inhalations of the morning air—something she never usually did—great lungfuls of air, like the way she sometimes breathed me in if I had been away for a while.

Back at the house, she lay on the couch, where she liked to lie after her walk, and I sat beside her and did a bit of work, the way I would usually sit beside her and work on the computer while she dozed.

When I first moved into my house about a decade ago, I planted rose bushes under the living room window, thinking that one day I would be able to open the window and have the scent of roses tumble into the house. And on this July day, I opened all the windows and the fragrance of the roses was all around us, just like I had once imagined it would be.

Charlotte wasn't eating at this point, but at dinnertime,

I ordered some takeout Italian food for my supper, and she broke her death fast to eat the meatballs in my pasta, taking each one delicately off the end of my fork. At night, we went up to bed as usual, with me following behind her on the stairs, listening to the familiar *thump-thump* of her feet on the risers. It seemed like any other day, but in the middle of the night, I woke to hear her panting, struggling to breathe, and knew that the sac around her heart had filled up again and that I would have to call the vet to come to the house in the morning.

When Charlotte was just over four months old, we moved together into this house. I brought hardly anything with me—dog stuff, some clothes, some kitchen implements, work things, a couch, and a mattress with bedding. I left my furniture and possessions in the house I was leaving, so it would show well as I was trying to sell it. Also, because it was easier to just have nothing, or next to nothing. It felt exactly where I was emotionally, as though I had lost everything.

And I had lost just about everything. My brother had died, and Hazel; I went through a breakup; another friend died; and a very close friend was diagnosed with terminal cancer—all within a six-month period.

But I had the new dog. Puppies have short attention spans, so when I painted the rooms in the house during those first few weeks, I was only able to do one wall a day before Charlotte bored of whatever diversion I had set up for her while I worked. But that was okay. I slowly painted the house and made it ours. At night, we lay on the mattress in the room I sleep in now and I watched the sky between the houses darken and lighten over the screen of distant trees.

Charlotte slept in my arms. She was young and she liked to have her heart overtop of mine so that our hearts could beat together, and to have her face pressed right up against my face. I imagine that this was what she was used to with her mother and littermates. It wasn't always comfortable for me, but I appreciated her need for physical closeness and put up with whatever discomfort I suffered because of it. She slept in my arms for years, three maybe four, and then one day moved off my bed to a bed on the floor.

Not long before she died, she and I were lying on my bed in the day, looking out at the space between the houses, and I noticed that we breathed at the same rate. Maybe our bodies were always naturally in rhythm, or maybe it had just come from years of being so intimately attached?

Every morning, for all the time we were together, Charlotte would jump up onto my bed to say good morning. She stayed there while I went to the bathroom, and when I came back, I'd get down on my knees in front of the bed and she'd muscle over on her stomach and press her head against my chest. It was a sign of happiness for her and it made her wag her tail. She pressed her head against me and I scratched her back. It always felt a bit weird to be on my knees in front of the bed every morning. My father had raised us as atheists, or perhaps agnostics—he believed that we are all just energy and that when we die, our energy attaches itself to the other energy that is around at the time—and I believe more or less what he believed. (He always hoped that his energy would attach to a tree after he died.) The morning ritual between Char and I was about reattaching to each other, being glad of each other, and I can see now that it was also a kind of prayer that we uttered together every morning, in devotion and in joy, before we got down to the serious business of the day—the business of living.

February 17

Fig is four months old today. She seems to have grown again. One of her bottom teeth is wobbling in its socket. Her back paws are as long as a jackrabbit's. After the morning walk today, she flopped across me and slept for hours. It was the kind of sleep that an adult dog has, not the fragmented, twitchy dozing of the puppy but the deep slumber of the mature canine. She seems bigger in every way and is biting less. The weird thing about all the puppy changes is that they seem to happen overnight, and even though I am watching all the time, their arrival is invisible.

I have decided to bring Fig back to puppy class for the next level. Even though she doesn't really learn anything and is constantly distracted, I think that is the point—that the distractions, in the form of other dogs and humans and loud noises and lots of activity, is what will be useful to her and gives her an accelerated kind of socialization that I just can't give her in our normal life. So, we will head back to the rubber-padded classroom on Tuesday afternoon, where, hopefully, we will meet a new batch of dogs.

The Fig that bites me less is a nice change. When she is sleepy, I can even put my hand in her mouth and feel around for the new teeth and she doesn't clamp down on my skin. She's not just resisting me. I'm not just annoyed by her antics.

After all her picky eating, Fig has finally settled on a raw dehydrated food that she will deign to eat without a topper of any sort. I still feed her the odd egg or bits of chicken and vegetables, but she will also eat the little dried pellets of food without anything on them, an important distinction if I am to ever leave her in the care of someone else who doesn't have the patience to cook her an egg or cut a chicken breast into tiny pieces for her. I have never met a dog like her, who eats and wants practically all human food. She even ate an orange segment the other day. None of my previous dogs, or indeed any dog I have ever known, has ever been interested in citrus fruits.

Another vet visit today for the last of her shots. I also had her microchipped while we were there—a weird thing to do to a living creature, but a precaution against her getting lost or, God forbid, stolen.

At four months old, Fig's heart rate is now 156 and she weighs twenty-nine pounds, which reinforces my idea that she will be a big dog. A typical female vizsla at maturity weighs between thirty-five and forty pounds. At four months old, Fig is almost at adult weight. If she grows twice as much again, which seems likely, she will top the scales at close to sixty pounds. Charlotte was a big vizsla also and weighed in at a pretty steady fifty-five pounds her whole life.

The pace of Fig's relentlessness is slowing. With writing, I often like to speed up the tempo, but with the puppy, I am very grateful it is slackening off.

When she was lying on me after the vet's, tired out from the excursion, I put my face against the top of her head and breathed her in—great lungfuls of her—the way that Charlotte had used to do to me. Fig liked this and wagged her tail. It felt good to know that this gesture of happiness could translate from my old dog to my new one, that I could keep this little piece of Charlotte going.

ENDINGS

My books are all bending towards nature now. I find that being with the dog in the forests and fields feels like "real life," in much the same way as the car wash had felt like real life when I was deciding whether or not to go to university at the beginning of my writing life. When I'm not in nature, I find myself thinking about the mysteries I have found there, or the profound experiences I have in that landscape.

Nature is as intense as love. One day, walking the dog by the river, I came upon a robin that was tangled in fishing line. The bird was hopping around on the grass, unable to fly because the line had wrapped around her wings. The only way to free the robin without damaging the feathers was to catch her and chew off the fishing line with my teeth while I held the Robin firmly in my hands to stop her from struggling and snaring herself further. It was an intense experience to have my mouth against the breast of the robin, gnawing away at the fishing line until I could free the bird and release it into the air. I could feel the fast fizz of the bird's heart against my lips.

I don't want to leave the world of nature, where so much of my imagination and senses are satisfied, where my curiosity is endlessly rampant.

I became a student of the river at my little cabin and wrote a book about what happened there. I followed the trail of wild apple trees and folded nature into a novel about World War II. *The River* and *The Ghost Orchard* were more or less non-fiction, but in the novel *The Evening Chorus*, I used my real experiences of nature to fuel the story, so even though the characters were fictional, all the bits about the natural world were taken from my own forays there when out with the dog.

Finally, inevitably, I guess, I also started to put the dog herself into my books, to write from exactly where I was. I decided to make my process transparent, to tell everything I knew about writing, and to start with the process, which meant starting where I was, on the couch with Charlotte at her end, in the middle of an August heat wave.

The novel *Machine Without Horses* is a book about writing. The first half is everything I consider when writing a novel, and the second half is the novel that results from those considerations. I meant it to be a sort of primer about writing, useful, I hope, to anyone starting out on the journey of being a writer, anyone who wants to know what goes into the writing of a novel.

It was liberating to sit on the couch in the heat wave, under the slow-turning ceiling fan, and write about sitting on the couch in the heat wave, etc.

I have been thinking a lot about writers and their dogs as I have been collecting the little stories to include in this book. What is interesting in the photos I have been finding of writers with their canine friends is how the people look antique, old-fashioned because of their clothes and hairstyles. But the dogs always look contemporary, because a dog is a dog is a dog, no matter the time and place. The dogs bridge the distance between worlds, and they look the same now as they did then. Ancient dogs could be modern dogs.

When I can recognize the look in Virginia Woolf's dog's

eyes as being a look I have seen on my own dog, Charlotte, I feel a greater connection to Woolf because of that. I can imagine her interactions with Grizzle as being similar to some of my interactions with Charlotte, and this extra knowledge eclipses the connection I already feel to her because I like her work. It is a stronger connection because it feels like it is happening in real time, in my time.

The loneliness of writing is confusing because writing is so immersive that in one way, it doesn't feel lonely at all. But this is deceptive. A writer friend of mine says that writing is so hard because we use the same parts of our brain to write as we do to handle our ordinary, daily communications. So, we're constantly shuffling language, reaching deeper, overriding ourselves. And, because we use language all the time to express ourselves, we can endlessly make our expression of it better. Writing can always be improved, and we could spend all of our time aiming towards a perfection of expression that is impossible to achieve. This is what makes it all-consuming, and also isolating.

Because of this, connection is all the more important.

One of my favourite small pleasures is the moment I am leaning behind my seat in the car and feeding my dog a biscuit, or when I am doing this on a walk, with the dog nosing into my palm and me slipping the biscuit between her two rows of teeth. In these moments, I am not looking at the dog, just doing everything by feel. It is an intimate act, to pass the biscuit past the dog's rubbery lips and to feel the serrated edges of her teeth as she takes the food into her mouth. The dog could so easily bite me, but she never does. She is always so gentle and I have come to trust in this gentleness, and it is the balance between what could happen and what does happen that gives me pleasure.

February 18

We went to the first class of the second level of puppy obedience despite my initial hesitation. There was a whole new roster of dogs, in a range of ages and sizes. Some dogs looked closer to adults than puppies. I think Fig is the youngest in attendance. There is what seems to be an adult pointer mix, who howls through all the instruction, and an enormous Labradoodle (What is happening to Labradoodles? They seem to be bred to be giants now), as well as some smaller mutts. We practised "stay" and then "down stay" to moderate success. Walking past the other dogs without pulling was much less successful.

There is no "Puppy Play" in this second level of classes. The dogs have to follow instruction for the whole hour. Interestingly, I found it more enjoyable than the first level of classes, where there was always some stress over what would happen during the "play." And it seems that, on first glance anyway, in this class there are no problem dogs.

The class is very good at exhausting Fig. She came home and fell asleep for two hours, lying on the couch beside me like a big dog while I was able to work on the computer.

I bought a harness for the car for Fig, after she repeatedly tried to launch herself into the front seat and twice succeeded. Also, she was getting into the habit of scrounging around on the floor of the back seat, pulling out anything that was under the seat and destroying it. She also liked to take the maps out of the string pockets on the back of the seats and shred them. But now, with the restraint, she is as good as can be. This is what I'm learning about Fig, that she needs a boundary and then, once it is in place, she is fine. It has taken me a while to learn this lesson because I keep comparing her to Charlotte, who never needed a boundary and just operated out of a kind of good sense, right from the beginning.

Really, it's a liability to me to keep comparing the two dogs, although forgivable, I guess. What I'm running up against so much in having the new puppy is my own resistance to realizing or acknowledging how different she is from my old dog. And that's the trouble with being older in general. There are inevitable comparisons in all things. I have had a lot of life experience at this point and I know, from this experience, that I prefer one thing over another.

IT IS THOUGHT that the bond between humans and dogs is especially strong because a dog is both mother and child to its person. The connection goes in both directions—being looked after by the dog in a maternal way, and looking after the dog in a way similar to how we care for our children.

The British editor and critic J.R. Ackerley wrote one of the most famous books about the bond between dogs and humans. *My Dog Tulip* was based on the passionate relationship he had with his German shepherd, Queenie, who for sixteen years was his beloved companion. The book describes, in candid detail, the years they were together, which Ackerley later said were the happiest of his life.

J.R. Ackerley and Queenie

Ackerley did not shy away from detailing every aspect of life with Queenie/Tulip, including lengthy passages about her heats and descriptions of how she looked while defecating. As anyone does when in love, he obsessed over the object of his affections. It just happens, in this case, that the object of his affections was not another human being, but a dog.

Queenie clearly thrived on the attention, living a long and healthy life. Ackerley baked her dog biscuits and left his job at the BBC early every day so that he could ensure she had a three-hour walk.

The dog, equally attached to Ackerley as he was to her, guarded him fiercely, barking at anyone who tried to enter any room he was in and not letting anyone come near him.

Ackerley's relationship with Queenie raises some interesting questions about love. Is it possible to fall in passionate love with a non-human animal? According to *My Dog Tulip*, it most definitely is.

The intimacy between a dog and their person is also about teaching them the world they will inhabit—your world, which will become theirs as they grow. This same process happens with children, but is less satisfying perhaps, because children often rebel against the world they know in order to gain autonomy and independence, to become themselves. They move away from your world, whereas dogs will happily move around with you there, and as long as they know what to expect from it, they will be happy in your world for their entire lives.

A new puppy comes as a feral creature, tearing round the house like a demon, testing everything with their mouth, oblivious to your sensible way of doing things.

But isn't it beautiful to teach her that singing means happiness, to welcome kisses on the top of her head, to swim and to ride in a car, to know the salty creaminess of a piece of cheese? Isn't it wonderful to relearn what is good in life myself, which comes forth under the guise of teaching the puppy how to be a good citizen in my world? It is so easy to disconnect from the very things we would say our life is about—love, joy, beauty, physical pleasure. It is shocking, in fact, how we can drift from the centre of ourselves without even noticing that it is happening.

But the puppy brings me back to the very essence of my life.

"This is a beach," I say to her. "You will like the feeling of the sand under your paws. Here is the warmth from fire. Here is a morsel of dried sausage."

Each new thing I introduce to her is something I know the value of, is something of meaning for me. So, at almost sixty, it feels a bit miraculous to make the world new again, for Fig and for myself.

ARE DOGS OF A MORE NOBLE nature than humans? Is that part of why we like being around them?

Alice Walker, in talking about her Labrador, Marley, wrote, "Dogs understand something I was late learning:

Alice Walker with her dog Miles

When we are mean to anyone or any being it is because we are temporarily not ourselves."[18]

Here's what I wonder: After a lifetime spent with dogs, where they have been the single biggest influence on my work and my life, do they make us better, or do they simply return us to who we are?

A dog pulls us from our work and often at a crucial moment, when the sentences are moving swiftly and fluently, when the interruption is not welcome. But out in the woods, the sun drifts through the trees like smoke, the ground smells metallic from the rain, the dog makes a crisp sound as she runs through the leaves. The book is forgotten. And while it seems that I couldn't possibly pick up where I left off, with that same concentration, when I return from the walk, the writing is full of energy and renewal.

February 20

Yesterday, it was a glorious and warm morning. There were robins in the trees in large numbers, the murmur of birdsong in the woods. Fig and I walked by ourselves in our usual place, and for the first time in ages, it wasn't a battle with the elements. As we were coming out of a patch of woods, we met a young couple with a big dog. Our dogs sniffed at each other and we humans had a little conversation, our version of sniffing.

The big, fluffy dog is only a year and a half. He is the first dog for the couple, and they went to all the puppy classes and worked hard at making him sociable and obedient.

"But," said the young woman, "we can never let him off leash because he just takes off. We've tried everything, but when he's free, he just keeps going."

"It's too bad," said the young man, "but we try to work around it. It's just how he is, and we can accommodate that."

Fig and I moved on, and I thought about that young couple and their dog for the whole walk.

They have the approach that nothing is perfect and that adjustments always need to be made, and this is the right approach to life and to all our relationships. But I am old enough, and lucky enough, to have had a few perfect things in my life. They never lasted long, but I recognized them for what they were when they appeared. Charlotte was one of these perfect things, and I think I have burdened my relationship with Fig by knowing this, and by knowing that Fig isn't perfect.

But as we walked through the woods, the puppy never going that far ahead of me, darting this way or that after a squirrel but always returning to the path and to me, I can see what a good dog she is. At four months, she is doing what many adult dogs aren't capable of doing. She is good at learning and has a cheerful, though stubborn, disposition. And most importantly, she has bonded to me and sees me as her person.

Ever since I began this puppy diary, I have been thinking about where I might end it. What would be the natural place to stop recording my experience of the new dog? I had thought that maybe I would write it until her adult teeth came in, or her eyes changed colour, or we finished the second level of puppy classes, or the season moved from winter into spring. I had thought that the place to end it was related to the dog's behaviour and growth. But now I can see that this is the right place to stop, and that it is not about the dog's growth at all, but about mine.

Every time I write a book, I have to discard everything I think I know about writing a book. What worked for one book usually doesn't work for another, and the freshness that is needed for the approach depends on feeling that the book you are working on is, in essence, the only important book. It is where you will say everything you need to say, and there is nothing to say beyond it. That's how you have to think about it in order for the writing of it to be new and full of energy.

So it is with the dog, it seems. In order to enjoy Fig, to be with her, I have to forget my other dogs—well, not so much forget them as not bring them into this moment.

So I won't.

Here we are, Fig and I, on this morning, walking through the snowy woods. Soon it will be spring, and she will have all her adult teeth, and her eyes will have changed colour, and she will have graduated from level two puppy class. And all of this isn't the end I had thought it would be, but the beginning.

Here we are, Fig and I, beginning.

Fig at eight weeks

Acknowledgements

Thanks to my agent, Clare Alexander, for your support and encouragement—and for your great love of dogs.

Working on this book with my stellar team of editors has been one of the best experiences of my writing life. Thank you, Jennifer Lambert (HarperCollins), Jenna Johnson (FSG), and Katie Bond (Aurum), for your joyful enthusiasm, and for all your fantastic suggestions that have made this a better book.

Thanks to Noelle Zitzer.

Thanks especially to Kathleen Winter.

Thanks to Mary Louise Adams, Karen Bayne, Anne Hardcastle, Catherine Humphreys, Frances Humphreys,

Judy Luck, Eleanor MacDonald, Kirsteen MacLeod, Susan Mockler, Susan Olding, Marco Reiter, Sarah Tsiang.

Thanks, Nancy—time with you and the dogs is the best of it.

Lastly, thanks to the dogs of now: Fig, Ranger, Violet, Henry, Holly.

And to the dogs of then: Kirsty, Lisa, Timmy, Hazel, Buddy, Mackay, Shadow, Esme, Charlotte. Oh, how we remember you.

Notes

1. Virginia Woolf, *The Diary of Virginia Woolf, Volume III*, edited by Anne Olivier Bell (London: The Hogarth Press, 1980), p. 62.

2. Virginia Woolf, letter to Vita Sackville-West, published in *The Letters of Virginia Woolf, Volume V*, edited by Nigel Nicolson and Joanne Trautmann (New York: Harcourt Brace Jovanovich, 1979), p. 396.

3. Virginia Woolf, *The Letters of Virginia Woolf, Volume III*, edited by Nigel Nicolson and Joanne Trautmann (New York: Harcourt Brace Jovanovich, 1978), p. 253.

4. Ibid., p. 303.

5. Virginia Woolf, "Gipsy, the Mongrel," *The Complete Shorter Fiction of Virginia Woolf*, edited by Susan Dick (New York: Harcourt, Inc., 1989), p. 274.

6. Ibid.

7. Ibid.

8. Ibid., p. 278.

9. Ibid.

10. Virginia Woolf, *Orlando* (London: Hogarth Press, 1928), p. 269.

11. E.B. White, "Bedfellows," *Essays of E.B. White* (New York: HarperCollins Publishers, 1956), p. 80.

12. Zora Neale Hurston, letter to Jean Parker, August 19, 1951, from *Zora Neale Hurston: A Life in Letters*, Carla Kaplan, ed. (New York: Doubleday, 2002), p. 675.

13. "Carlo (1849–1866), dog," Emily Dickinson Museum website, https://www.emilydickinsonmuseum.org/carlo-1849-1866-dog/.

14. Letter from Emily Dickinson to T.W. Higginson, February 1863, https://www.emilydickinsonmuseum.org/carlo-1849-1866-dog/.

15. Mary Oliver, *Dog Songs* (New York: Penguin Press, 2013), p. 119.

16. Dinesen, Isak, *Out of Africa* (New York: Vintage, 1989), p. 80.

17. Agatha Christie, *Dumb Witness* (London: Collins Crime Club, 1937), p. 4.

18. Alice Walker, "Crimes Against Dog," *We Are the Ones We Have Been Waiting For* (New York: The New Press, 2006), p. 80.

Illustration Credits

Throughout (pages 1, 53, 81, 121, 137, 191, and 229): Lab vectors by Vecteezy.

p. 1: Painting by Na Kim.

p. 67: Grizzle, in a photograph taken by Virginia Woolf. MS Thr 564 (155). Houghton Library, Harvard University. Used with permission.

p. 70: Thomas Hardy with Wessex. Dorset County Museum, Dorchester, UK. Used with permission.

p. 73: E.B. White and one of his dachshunds, Minnie. Copyright © by E.B. White. Reprinted in *E.B. White on Dogs*, edited by Martha White. Reprinted by permission of ICM Partners.

p. 76: James Thurber's dog Muggs. Photograph, c. 1920, courtesy of Rosemary A. Thurber.

p. 108: Gertrude Stein holding a portrait of Basket while the real Basket looks on. Yale Collection of American Literature, Beinecke Rare Book & Manuscript Library, Yale University. Used with permission.

p. 110: Maurice Sendak and Herman. Copyright © Mariana Cook 2005.

p. 113: Painting of Keeper by Emily Brontë, 1838. Watercolour. Brontë Parsonage Museum.

p. 117: Zora Neale Hurston with friends and one of her dogs. Zora Neale Hurston Papers, Special and Area Studies Collections, George A. Smathers Libraries, University of Florida, Gainesville, FL. Used with permission.

p. 128: Virginia Woolf's novel *Flush*, with her dog Pinka on the cover. Artwork from *Flush: A Biography* by Virginia Woolf, published by Chatto & Windus. Copyright © the Trustees of the Virginia Woolf Estate. Reprinted by permission of The Random House Group Limited.

p. 149: "The Newfoundland Dog." Engraving by James Hope Stewart, c. 1834. Public domain.

p. 150: Mary Oliver and Percy. Copyright © 2005 by Rachel Giese Brown. Used with permission.

p. 163: Anton Chekhov and Khina. P.I. Seryogin, 1897. Public domain.

p. 177: Karen Blixen and her deerhounds. Photographer unknown. Photo in the Karen Blixen archive at the Royal Danish Library. Used with permission.

p. 186: Alexander Pope and his dog Bounce. Painting by Jonathan Richardson (British, 1665–1745), c. 1718. Oil on canvas. Reproduced courtesy of Bridgeman Images, London, UK.

A Note About the Author

Helen Humphreys is an acclaimed award-winning author of fiction, nonfiction, and poetry. Her work includes the novels *The Evening Chorus*, *Coventry*, and *Afterimage*, and the nonfiction books *The Ghost Orchard* and *The Frozen Thames*. She has won the Rogers Writers' Trust Fiction Prize and the Toronto Book Award, and has been a finalist for the Governor General's Literary Award for Fiction, the Trillium Book Award, the Lambda Literary Award, and CBC Radio's Canada Reads.